Super Quick Ninja Dual Zone
AIR FRYER
COOKBOOK FOR UK

1800+ Days of Delicious, Mouthwatering & Time-Saving Book for Beginners - Ready in 30 Minutes or Less

Camila Pinto Ferreira

Copyright© 2024 By Camila Pinto Ferreira

All rights reserved worldwide.

No part of this book may be reproduced or transmitted in any form or by any means, electronic or mechanical, including photo- copying, recording or by any information storage and retrieval system, without written permission from the publisher, except for the inclusion of brief quotations in a review.

Warning-Disclaimer

The purpose of this book is to educate and entertain. The author or publisher does not guarantee that anyone following the techniques, suggestions, tips, ideas, or strategies will become successful. The author and publisher shall have neither liability or responsibility to anyone with respect to any loss or damage caused, or alleged to be caused, directly or indirectly by the information contained in this book.

TABLE OF CONTENTS

1	Introduction	
4	Chapter 1	Breakfasts
12	Chapter 2	Family Favorites
16	Chapter 3	Fast and Easy Everyday Favourites
20	Chapter 4	Beef, Pork, and Lamb
31	Chapter 5	Fish and Seafood
40	Chapter 6	Poultry
49	Chapter 7	Snacks and Starters
56	Chapter 8	Vegetables and Sides
63	Chapter 9	Vegetarian Mains
67	Chapter 10	Desserts
71	Appendix 1:	Basic Kitchen Conversions & Equivalents
72	Appendix 2:	Recipes Index

INTRODUCTION

Welcome to the next generation of cooking innovation with the Ninja Dual zone Air Fryer. As technology continues to evolve, so does our approach to preparing delicious meals quickly and efficiently. The Ninja Dual zone Air Fryer represents the pinnacle of air frying technology, offering unmatched versatility, convenience, and precision to elevate your culinary creations to new heights.

Unleashing the Power of Air Frying

Air frying has emerged as a popular cooking method for health-conscious individuals seeking to enjoy the crispy, flavorful goodness of fried foods without the excess oil and calories. With the Ninja Dual zone Air Fryer, you can indulge in all your favorite fried treats guilt-free, thanks to its advanced air frying technology that circulates hot air around your food to produce a crispy, golden exterior with a tender, juicy interior.

Dual zone Cooking for Maximum Versatility

What sets the Ninja Dual zone Air Fryer apart is its innovative dual-zone cooking capability, allowing you to cook two separate dishes simultaneously at different temperatures and times. Whether you're preparing a savory main course and a side dish or hosting a dinner party with a variety of appetizers, the dual-zone feature provides unparalleled flexibility to accommodate multiple dishes with ease.

Precision Control at Your Fingertips

Equipped with intuitive digital controls and customizable cooking presets, the Ninja Dual zone Air Fryer puts precision cooking at your fingertips. With just the touch of a button, you can select the ideal cooking temperature and time for each zone, ensuring perfect results every time. Whether you're frying, roasting, baking, or dehydrating, the Ninja Dual zone Air Fryer takes the guesswork out of cooking, so you can focus on creating delicious meals with confidence.

Sleek Design, Superior Performance

Designed with both style and functionality in mind, the Ninja Dual zone Air Fryer features a sleek, modern design that complements any kitchen decor. Its compact footprint makes it ideal for small spaces, while its spacious cooking capacity ensures you can prepare meals for the whole family. With its powerful performance and effortless operation, the Ninja Dual zone Air Fryer is the ultimate kitchen companion for busy home cooks and culinary enthusiasts alike.

Tips for Making the Most of Your Ninja Dual zone Air Fryer

1.Preheat Your Air Fryer: Just like with traditional ovens, preheating your air fryer can help ensure even cooking and crispy results. Preheat your Ninja Dual zone Air Fryer for a few minutes before adding your food for optimal performance.

2.Use the Dual zone Feature: Take advantage of the dual-zone cooking capability of your air fryer by cooking two different dishes simultaneously at different temperatures and times. This feature allows you to save time and prepare a complete meal all at once.

3.Rotate and Flip: For even cooking, rotate and flip your food halfway through the cooking process. This ensures that all sides of your food are evenly exposed to the circulating hot air, resulting in a uniformly crispy exterior and tender interior.

4.Don't Overcrowd the Basket: To achieve the best air frying results, avoid overcrowding the basket of your air fryer. Leave some space between each piece of food to allow for proper air circulation and ensure that your food cooks evenly.

5. Experiment with Different Temperatures and Times: Every recipe is different, so don't be afraid to experiment with different cooking temperatures and times to find what works best for your favorite dishes. Start with the recommended settings and adjust as needed based on your preferences and the results you're aiming for.

6. Use Oil Sparingly: While air frying requires much less oil than traditional frying methods, a light coating of oil can help enhance the crispiness of your food and prevent it from sticking to the basket. Use a high-quality cooking spray or brush your food with a small amount of oil before air frying.

7. Clean Your Air Fryer Regularly: To maintain optimal performance and prolong the life of your Ninja Dual zone Air Fryer, be sure to clean it regularly. Follow the manufacturer's instructions for cleaning and care, and remove any food residue or grease buildup after each use.

8. Get Creative: Don't limit yourself to just frying! Your air fryer is a versatile kitchen appliance that can be used for a wide range of cooking methods, including roasting, baking, grilling, and even dehydrating. Get creative with your recipes and explore the endless possibilities of air frying.

9. Monitor Your Food: Keep an eye on your food as it cooks to prevent it from overcooking or burning. Use the viewing window or lift the basket to check on your food periodically and make any necessary adjustments to the cooking time or temperature.

10. Have Fun: Most importantly, have fun experimenting with your Ninja Dual zone Air Fryer! Embrace the convenience and versatility of air frying, and enjoy creating delicious, healthier versions of your favorite foods with ease.

In conclusion, the Ninja Dual zone Air Fryer cookbook is your go-to resource for maximizing the potential of your air fryer. With a variety of recipes, helpful tips, and innovative features like dual-zone cooking, this cookbook offers endless possibilities for creating delicious, healthier meals with ease. Whether you're new to air frying or a seasoned chef, the cookbook is sure to become an essential tool in your kitchen, inspiring you to explore the world of air frying and unleash your culinary creativity.

Chapter 1
Breakfasts

Chapter 1 Breakfasts

Simple Scotch Eggs

Prep time: 5 minutes | Cook time: 25 minutes | Serves 4

- 4 large hard boiled eggs
- 1 (340 g) package pork banger meat
- 8 slices streaky bacon
- 4 wooden cocktail sticks, soaked in water for at least 30 minutes

1. Slice the banger meat into four parts and place each part into a large circle. 2. Put an egg into each circle and wrap it in the banger. Put in the refrigerator for 1 hour. 3. Preheat the air fryer to 230ºC. 4. Make a cross with two pieces of streaky bacon. Put a wrapped egg in the center, fold the bacon over top of the egg, and secure with a toothpick. 5. Select zone 1, select AIR FRY, set temperature to 230ºC, and set time to 25 minutes. Press the START/PAUSE button to begin cooking. 6. Serve immediately.

Baked Egg and Mushroom Cups

Prep time: 5 minutes | Cook time: 15 minutes | Serves 6

- rapeseed oil cooking spray
- 6 large eggs
- 1 garlic clove, minced
- ½ teaspoon salt
- ½ teaspoon black pepper
- Pinch red pepper flakes
- 230 g baby mushrooms, sliced
- 235 g fresh baby spinach
- 2 spring onions, white parts and green parts, diced

1. Preheat the air fryer to 160ºC. Lightly coat the inside of six silicone muffin cups or a six-cup muffin tin with rapeseed oil cooking spray. 2. In a large bowl, beat the eggs, garlic, salt, pepper, and red pepper flakes for 1 to 2 minutes, or until well combined. 3. Fold in the mushrooms, spinach, and spring onions. 4. Divide the mixture evenly among the muffin cups. 5. Place into the zone 1 and zone 2 air fryer baskets. 6. Select zone 1, select BAKE, set temperature to 200ºC, and set time to 12 - 15 minutes. Next, press MATCH COOK to match zone 2 settings to zone 1. Finally, press START/PAUSE to initiate the cooking process. 7. Remove and allow to cool for 5 minutes before serving.

Breakfast Meatballs

Prep time: 10 minutes | Cook time: 15 minutes | Makes 18 meatballs

- 450 g pork banger meat, removed from casings
- ½ teaspoon salt
- ¼ teaspoon ground black pepper
- 120 g grated mature Cheddar cheese
- 30 g soft cheese, softened
- 1 large egg, whisked

1. Combine all ingredients in a large bowl. Form mixture into eighteen 1-inch meatballs. 2. Place meatballs into the two ungreased zone 1 and zone 2 air fryer baskets. 3. Select zone 1, Select AIR FRY, set temperature to 200ºC , set time to 15 minutes. Then press MATCH COOK, match zone 2 settings to zone 1. Finally, Press START/PAUSE to begin. Shaking basket three times during cooking. Meatballs will be browned on the outside and have an internal temperature of at least 64ºC when completely cooked. 4. Serve warm.

Easy Buttermilk Biscuits

Prep time: 5 minutes | Cook time: 18 minutes | Makes 16 biscuits

- 300 g plain flour
- 1 tablespoon baking powder
- 1 teaspoon coarse or flaky salt
- 1 teaspoon sugar
- ½ teaspoon baking soda
- 8 tablespoons (1 stick) unsalted butter, at room temperature
- 235 ml buttermilk, chilled

1. Stir together the flour, baking powder, salt, sugar, and baking powder in a large bowl. 2. Add the butter and stir to mix well. Pour in the buttermilk and stir with a rubber spatula just until incorporated. 3. Place the dough onto a lightly floured surface and roll the dough out to a disk, ½ inch thick. Cut out the biscuits with a 2-inch round cutter and re-roll any scraps until you have 16 biscuits. 4. Preheat the air fryer to 160ºC. 5. Working in batches, arrange the biscuits in both baskets in a single layer. 6. Select zone 1, select BAKE, set temperature to 160ºC, set time to 18 minutes. Then press MATCH COOK to match zone 2 setting with zone 1. Finally, press START/PAUSE to begin cooking until the biscuits are golden brown. 7. Remove from the basket to a plate and repeat with the remaining biscuits. Serve hot.

Baked Potato Breakfast Boats

Prep time: 10 minutes | Cook time: 20 minutes | Serves 4

- 2 large white potatoes, scrubbed
- rapeseed oil
- Salt and freshly ground black pepper, to taste
- 4 eggs
- 2 tablespoons chopped, cooked bacon
- 235 g grated Cheddar cheese

1. Poke holes in the potatoes with a fork and microwave on full power for 5 minutes. 2. Turn potatoes over and cook an additional 3 to 5 minutes, or until the potatoes are fork-tender. 3. Cut the potatoes in half lengthwise and use a spoon to scoop out the inside of the potato. Be careful to leave a layer of potato so that it makes a sturdy "boat." 4. Preheat the air fryer to 180ºC. 5. Lightly spray the zone 1 and zone 2 air fryer baskets with rapeseed oil. Spray the skin side of the potatoes with oil and sprinkle with salt and pepper to taste. 6. Place the potato skins in the zone 1 and zone 2 air fryer baskets, skin-side down. Crack one egg into each potato skin. 7. Sprinkle ½ tablespoon of bacon pieces and 60 ml grated cheese on top of each egg. Sprinkle with salt and pepper to taste. 8. Select zone 1, select BAKE, set the temperature to 180 ºC. Set time to 5-6 minutes or 7-8 minutes depends on your favourite. Next, press MATCH COOK to match zone 2 settings to zone 1. Finally, Press START/PAUSE to begin cooking.

Drop Biscuits

Prep time: 10 minutes | Cook time: 9 to 10 minutes | Serves 5

- 500 g plain flour
- 1 tablespoon baking powder
- 1 tablespoon sugar (optional)
- 1 teaspoon salt
- 6 tablespoons butter, plus more for brushing on the biscuits (optional)
- 180 ml buttermilk
- 1 to 2 tablespoons oil

1. In a large bowl, whisk the flour, baking powder, sugar (if using), and salt until blended. 2. Add the butter. Using a pastry cutter or 2 forks, work the dough until pea-size balls of the butter-flour mixture appear. Stir in the buttermilk until the mixture is sticky. 3. Preheat the air fryer to 170ºC. Line the zone 1 and zone 2 air fryer baskets with parchment paper and spritz it with oil. 4. Drop the dough by the tablespoonful onto the prepared zone 1 and zone 2 baskets, leaving 1 inch between each, to form 10 biscuits. 5. Select zone 1, select BAKE, set the temperature to 170ºC. Set time to 5 minutes. Next, press MATCH COOK to match zone 2 settings to zone 1. Then press START/PAUSE to begin cooking. 6. After 5 minutes, press PAUSE button to pause the air fryer, then flip the biscuits. Reinsert drawer in units, set time to 4 minutes and press START/PAUSE to resume cooking to get a light brown top. You may cook 5 minutes more for a darker biscuit depends on your favourite. Brush the tops with melted butter, if desired.

Egg in a Hole

Prep time: 5 minutes | Cook time: 5 minutes | Serves 1

- 1 slice bread
- 1 teaspoon butter, softened
- 1 egg
- Salt and pepper, to taste
- 1 tablespoon grated Cheddar cheese
- 2 teaspoons diced gammon

1. Preheat the air fryer to 170ºC. Place a baking dish in the zone 1 air fryer basket. 2. On a flat work surface, cut a hole in the center of the bread slice with a 2½-inch-diameter biscuit cutter. 3. Spread the butter evenly on each side of the bread slice and transfer to the baking dish. 4. Crack the egg into the hole and season as desired with salt and pepper. Scatter the grated cheese and diced gammon on top. 5. Select zone1, select BAKE, set temperature to 170ºC, set time to 5 minutes. Finally, press START/PAUSE to begin cooking until the bread is lightly browned and the egg is cooked to your preference. 6. Remove from the basket and serve hot.

Chimichanga Breakfast Burrito

Prep time: 10 minutes | Cook time: 10 minutes | Serves 2

- 2 large (10- to 12-inch) wheat maize wraps
- 120 g canned refried beans (pinto or black work equally well)
- 4 large eggs, cooked scrambled
- 4 maize maize wrap chips, crushed
- 120 g grated chilli cheese
- 12 pickled jalapeño slices
- 1 tablespoon vegetable oil
- Guacamole, tomato salsa, and sour cream, for serving (optional)

1. Place the maize wraps on a work surface and divide the refried beans between them, spreading them in a rough rectangle in the center of the maize wraps. Top the beans with the scrambled eggs, crushed chips, cheese, and jalapeños. Fold one side over the fillings, then fold in each short side and roll up the rest of the way like a burrito. 2. Brush the outside of the burritos with the oil, then transfer to the air fryer, seam-side down. 3. Select zone 1, select AIR FRY, set temperature to 180ºC, and set time to 10 minutes. Press the START/PAUSE button to begin until the maize wraps are browned and crisp and the filling is warm throughout. 4. Transfer the chimichangas to plates and serve warm with guacamole, tomato salsa, and sour cream, if you like.

Chapter 1 Breakfasts

Spinach and Mushroom Mini Quiche

Prep time: 10 minutes | Cook time: 15 minutes | Serves 4

- 1 teaspoon rapeseed oil, plus more for spraying
- 235 g roughly chopped mushrooms
- 235 g fresh baby spinach, grated
- 4 eggs, beaten
- 120 g grated Cheddar cheese
- 120 g grated Cheddar cheese
- ¼ teaspoon salt
- ¼ teaspoon black pepper

1. Spray 4 silicone baking cups with rapeseed oil and set aside. 2. In a medium sauté pan over medium heat, warm 1 teaspoon of rapeseed oil. Add the mushrooms and sauté until soft, 3 to 4 minutes. 3. Add the spinach and cook until wilted, 1 to 2 minutes. Set aside. 4. In a medium bowl, whisk together the eggs, Cheddar cheese, Cheddar cheese, salt, and pepper. 5. Gently fold the mushrooms and spinach into the egg mixture. 6. Pour ¼ of the mixture into each silicone baking cup. 7. Place the baking cups into the zone 1 and zone 2 air fryer baskets. 8. Select zone 1, Select BAKE, set temperature to 180ºC, set time to 5 minutes, then press MATCH COOK, match zone 2 settings to zone 1. Finally, Press START/PAUSE to begin cooking. 9. After 5 minutes, press PAUSE button to pause the air fryer. Stir the mixture in each ramekin slightly and reinsert the baskets, then set time to 3-5 minutes. Then press MATCH COOK, match zone 2 settings to zone 1. Finally, press START/PAUSE to continue cooking until the egg has set.

Breakfast Cobbler

Prep time: 20 minutes | Cook time: 30 minutes | Serves 4

Filling:
- 280 g banger meat, crumbled
- 60 g minced onions
- 2 cloves garlic, minced
- ½ teaspoon fine sea salt
- ½ teaspoon ground black pepper
- 1 (230 g) package soft cheese (or soft cheese style spread for dairy-free), softened
- 180 g beef or chicken stock

Biscuits:
- 3 large egg whites
- 90 g blanched almond flour
- 1 teaspoon baking powder
- ¼ teaspoon fine sea salt
- 2½ tablespoons very cold unsalted butter, cut into ¼-inch pieces
- Fresh thyme leaves, for garnish

1. Preheat the air fryer to 200ºC. 2. Place the banger, onions, and garlic in the pie dishes. Using your hands, break up the banger into small pieces and spread it evenly throughout the pie dishes. Season with the salt and pepper. Place the pans in the zone 1 and zone 2 air fryers. 3. Select zone 1, Select BAKE, set temperature to 200ºC, set time to 5 minutes, then press MATCH COOK to match zone 2 setting with zone 1. Press START/PAUSE to begin cooking. 4. While the banger cooks, place the soft cheese and stock in a food processor or blender and purée until smooth. 5. Press PAUSE button to pause the zone 1 and zone 2 air fryers. Remove the pork from the air fryer and use a fork or metal spatula to crumble it more. Pour the soft cheese mixture into the banger and stir to combine. Set aside. 6. Make the biscuits: Place the egg whites in a medium-sized mixing bowl or the bowl of a stand mixer and whip with a hand mixer or stand mixer until stiff peaks form. 7. In a separate medium-sized bowl, whisk together the almond flour, baking powder, and salt, then cut in the butter. When you are done, the mixture should still have chunks of butter. Gently fold the flour mixture into the egg whites with a rubber spatula. 8. Use a large spoon or ice cream scoop to scoop the dough into 4 equal-sized biscuits, making sure the butter is evenly distributed. 9. Place the biscuits on top of the banger. Select zone 1, Select BAKE, set temperature to 200ºC, set time to 5 minutes, then press MATCH COOK to match zone 2 setting with zone 1. Press START/PAUSE to begin cooking. 10. After 5 minutes, turn the temperature down to 160º, set time to 17-20 minutes, then press MATCH COOK to match zone 2 setting with zone 1. Finally press START/PAUSE to continue cooking until the biscuits are golden brown. Serve garnished with fresh thyme leaves. 11. Store leftovers in an airtight container in the refrigerator for up to 3 days. Reheat in a preheated 180ºC air fryer for 5 minutes, or until warmed through.

Quick and Easy Blueberry Muffins

Prep time: 10 minutes | Cook time: 12 minutes | Makes 8 muffins

- 160 g flour
- 96 g sugar
- 2 teaspoons baking powder
- ¼ teaspoon salt
- 80 ml rapeseed oil
- 1 egg
- 120 ml milk
- 160 g blueberries, fresh or frozen and thawed

1. Preheat the air fryer to 170ºC. 2. In a medium bowl, stir together flour, sugar, baking powder, and salt. 3. In a separate bowl, combine oil, egg, and milk and mix well. 4. Add egg mixture to dry ingredients and stir just until moistened. 5. Gently stir in the blueberries. 6. Spoon batter evenly into parchment paper-lined muffin cups. 7. Put muffin cups in zone 1 and zone 2 air fryer baskets. 8. Select zone 1, select BAKE, set temperature to 170ºC, set time to 12 minutes. Then press MATCH COOK to match zone 2 setting to zone 1. Finally, press START/PAUSE to begin cooking until tops spring back when touched lightly. 9. Serve immediately.

Eggy Bread Sticks

Prep time: 10 minutes | Cook time: 9 minutes | Serves 4

- Oil, for spraying
- 6 large eggs
- 315 ml milk
- 2 teaspoons vanilla extract
- 1 teaspoon ground cinnamon
- 8 slices bread, cut into thirds
- Syrup of choice, for serving

1. Preheat the air fryer to 190ºC. Line the zone 1 and zone 2 air fryer baskets with parchment and spray lightly with oil. 2. In a shallow bowl, whisk the eggs, milk, vanilla, and cinnamon. 3. Dunk one piece of bread in the egg mixture, making sure to coat both sides. Work quickly so the bread doesn't get soggy. Immediately transfer the bread to the prepared basket. 4. Repeat with the remaining bread, making sure the pieces don't touch each other. You may need to use zone 1 and zone2 to bake the sticks. 5. Select zone 1, select BAKE, set temperature to 190ºC, and set time to 5 minutes. Next, press MATCH COOK to match zone 2 settings to zone 1. Finally, press START/PAUSE to begin.6. After 5 minutes, press PAUSE button to pause the air fryer. Then flip them. Reinsert the drawers in units. Set time to 3-4 minutes, press MATCH COOK to match zone 2 settings to zone 1. Then press START/PAUSE to resume cooking until browned and crispy. 7. Serve immediately with your favourite syrup.

All-in-One Toast

Prep time: 10 minutes | Cook time: 10 minutes | Serves 1

- 1 strip bacon, diced
- 1 slice 1-inch thick bread
- 1 egg
- Salt and freshly ground black pepper, to taste
- 60 g grated Monterey Jack or Chedday cheese

1. Select zone 1, select AIR FRY, set temperature to 200ºC, and set time to 3 minutes, then press START/PAUSE to air fry the bacon; shaking the basket once or twice while it cooks. Then Press Pause button to pause the zone 1 air fryer. Remove the bacon to a paper towel lined plate and set aside. 2. Use a sharp paring knife to score a large circle in the middle of the slice of bread, cutting halfway through, but not all the way through to the cutting board. Press down on the circle in the center of the bread slice to create an indentation. 3. Transfer the slice of bread, hole side up, to the air fryer basket. Crack the egg into the center of the bread, and season with salt and pepper. 4. Select zone 1, select AIR FRY, set temperature to 190ºC, and set time to 5 minutes, then press START/PAUSE to begin. Sprinkle the grated cheese around the edges of the bread, leaving the center of the yolk uncovered, and top with the cooked bacon. Press the cheese and bacon into the bread lightly to help anchor it to the bread and prevent it from blowing around in the air fryer. 5. Air fry for one or two more minutes, just to melt the cheese and finish cooking the egg.

Potatoes Lyonnaise

Prep time: 10 minutes | Cook time: 31 minutes | Serves 4

- 1 sweet/mild onion, sliced
- 1 teaspoon butter, melted
- 1 teaspoon soft brown sugar
- 2 large white potatoes (about 450 g in total), sliced ½-inch thick
- 1 tablespoon vegetable oil
- Salt and freshly ground black pepper, to taste

1. Preheat the air fryer to 190ºC. 2. Toss the sliced onions, melted butter and soft brown sugar together in the air fryer basket. Select zone 1, select AIR FRY, set temperature to 190ºC, set time to 8 minutes. Next, press MATCH COOK to match zone 2 setting to zone 1. Then, press START/PAUSE to begin. Shaking the basket occasionally to help the onions cook evenly. 3. While the onions are cooking, bring a saucepan of salted water to a boil on the stovetop. Par-cook the potatoes in boiling water for 3 minutes. Drain the potatoes and pat them dry with a clean kitchen towel. 4. Press PAUSE button to pause zone 1 and zone 2. Add the potatoes to the onions in the air fryer baskets and drizzle with vegetable oil. Toss to coat the potatoes with the oil and season with salt and freshly ground black pepper. 5. Select zone 1, select AIR FRY, increase the temperature to 200°C, and set time to 20 minutes. Next, press MATCH COOK to match zone 2 settings to zone 1. Press START/PAUSE to initiate the cooking process. Tossing the vegetables a few times during the cooking time to help the potatoes brown evenly. 6. Season with salt and freshly ground black pepper and serve warm.

Jalapeño Popper Egg Cups

Prep time: 10 minutes | Cook time: 10 minutes | Serves 2

- 4 large eggs
- 60 g chopped pickled jalapeños
- 60 g full-fat soft cheese
- 120 g grated mature Cheddar cheese

1. In a medium bowl, beat the eggs, then pour into four silicone muffin cups. 2. In a large microwave-safe bowl, place jalapeños, soft cheese, and Cheddar. Microwave for 30 seconds and stir. Take a spoonful, approximately ¼ of the mixture, and place it in the center of one of the egg cups. Repeat with remaining mixture. 3. Place egg cups into the air fryer basket. 4. Select zone 1, select BAKE, set temperature to 160ºC, and set time to 10 minutes. Then press START/PAUSE to begin cooking. 5. Serve warm.

Chapter 1 Breakfasts

Cinnamon-Raisin Bagels

Prep time: 30 minutes | Cook time: 10 minutes | Makes 4 bagels

- Oil, for spraying
- 60 g raisins
- 120 g self-raising flour, plus more for dusting
- 235 ml natural yoghurt
- 1 teaspoon ground cinnamon
- 1 large egg

1. Line the zone 1 and zone 2 air fryer baskets with parchment and spray lightly with oil. 2. Place the raisins in a bowl of hot water and let sit for 10 to 15 minutes, until they have plumped. This will make them extra juicy. 3. In a large bowl, mix together the flour, yoghurt, and cinnamon with your hands or a large silicone spatula until a ball is formed. It will be quite sticky for a while. 4. Drain the raisins and gently work them into the ball of dough. 5. Place the dough on a lightly floured work surface and divide into 4 equal pieces. Roll each piece into an 8- or 9-inch-long rope and shape it into a circle, pinching the ends together to seal. 6. In a small bowl, whisk the egg. Brush the egg onto the tops of the dough. 7. Place the dough in the prepared zone 1 and zone 2 baskets. 8. Select zone 1 , select BAKE, set temperature to 180ºC, set time to 10 minutes. Then press MATCH COOK, match zone 2 settings to zone 1. Finally, Press START/PAUSE to begin cooking. 9. Serve immediately.

Bacon Cheese Egg with Avocado & Blueberry Cobbler

Prep time: 15 minutes | Cook time: 20 minutes

Bacon Chess Egg with Avocado | Serves 4

- 6 large eggs
- 60 ml double cream
- 350 g chopped cauliflower
- 235 g grated medium Cheddar cheese
- 1 medium avocado, peeled and pitted
- 8 tablespoons full-fat sour cream
- 2 spring onions, sliced on the bias
- 12 lices bacon, cooked and crumbled

Blueberry Cobbler | Serves 4

- 40 g wholemeal pastry flour
- ¾ teaspoon baking powder
- Dash sea salt
- 120 ml semi-skimmed milk
- 2 tablespoons pure maple syrup
- ½ teaspoon vanilla extract
- Cooking oil spray
- 120 g fresh blueberries
- 60 g muesli

Prepare for Bacon Chess Egg with Avocado (zone 1):

1.In a medium bowl, whisk eggs and cream together. Pour into a round baking dish. 2. Add cauliflower and mix, then top with Cheddar. Place dish into zone 1.

Prepare for Blueberry Cobbler (zone 2) :

1. In a medium bowl, whisk the flour, baking powder, and salt. Add the milk, maple syrup, and vanilla and gently whisk, just until thoroughly combined. 2. Spray a 6-by-2-inch round baking pan with cooking oil and pour the batter into the pan. Top evenly with the blueberries and muesli. 3. place the pan into the zone 2.

Cook:

1.Finally, select zone 1, Select BAKE, set temperature to 160ºC, set time to 20 minutes. Select zone2, select BAKE, set the temperature to 180ºC, and set the time to 15 minutes. Then press SMART COOK. Press START/PAUSE to begin cooking. The two dishes will complete in the same time. 2. For zone 1, when completely cooked, eggs will be firm and cheese will be browned. Slice into four pieces. 3. Slice avocado and divide evenly among pieces. Top each piece with 2 tablespoons sour cream, sliced spring onions, and crumbled bacon. 4. For zone 2, When the cooking is complete, the cobbler should be nicely browned and a knife inserted into the middle should come out clean. Enjoy plain or topped with a little vanilla yoghurt.

Honey-Apricot Muesli with Greek Yoghurt

Prep time: 10 minutes | Cook time: 30 minutes | Serves 6

- 235 g porridge oats
- 60 g dried apricots, diced
- 60 g almond slivers
- 60 g walnuts, chopped
- 60 g pumpkin seeds
- 60 to 80 ml honey, plus more for drizzling
- 1 tablespoon rapeseed oil
- 1 teaspoon ground cinnamon
- ¼ teaspoon ground nutmeg
- ¼ teaspoon salt
- 2 tablespoons sugar-free dark chocolate crisps (optional)
- 700 ml fat-free natural yoghurt

1. Preheat the air fryer to 130ºC. Line zone 1 and zone 2 air fryer baskets with parchment paper. 2. In a large bowl, combine the oats, apricots, almonds, walnuts, pumpkin seeds, honey, rapeseed oil, cinnamon, nutmeg, and salt, mixing so that the honey, oil, and spices are well distributed. 3. Pour the mixture onto the parchment paper and spread it into an even layer. 4. Select zone 1, select AIR FRY, set temperature to130ºC , set time to 10 minutes. Then press MATCH COOK to match zone 2 setting with zone 1. Initiate the cooking process by pressing START/PAUSE. 5. Press the Pause button to pause the air fryer. Then shake or stir and spread back out into an even layer. set time to 10 minutes. Then press MATCH COOK to match zone 2 setting with zone 1. Press START/PAUSE to continue. 6. Then repeat the process of shaking or stirring the mixture. Bake for an additional 10 minutes before removing from the air fryer. 7. Allow the muesli to cool completely before stirring in the chocolate crisps (if using) and pouring into an airtight container for storage. 8. For each serving, top 120 ml Greek yoghurt with 80 ml muesli and a drizzle of honey, if needed.

Strawberry Toast

Prep time: 10 minutes | Cook time: 8 minutes | Makes 4 toasts

- 4 slices bread, ½-inch thick
- Butter-flavoured cooking spray
- 235 g sliced strawberries
- 1 teaspoon sugar

1. Spray one side of each bread slice with butter-flavoured cooking spray. Lay slices sprayed side down. 2. Divide the strawberries among the bread slices. 3. Sprinkle evenly with the sugar and place in the zone 1 and zone 2 air fryer baskets in a single layer. 4. Select zone 1, Select BAKE, set temperature to 200ºC, set time to 8 minutes. Then press MATCH COOK, match zone 2 settings to zone 1. Finally, Press START/PAUSE to begin cooking. The bottom should look brown and crisp and the top should look glazed.

Asparagus and Pepper Strata & Easy Banger Pizza

Prep time: 20 minutes | Cook time: 14 to 20 minutes

Asparagus and Pepper Strata | Serves 4

- 8 large asparagus spears, trimmed and cut into 2-inch pieces
- 80 g grated carrot
- 120 g chopped red pepper
- 2 slices wholemeal bread, cut into ½-inch cubes
- 3 egg whites
- 1 egg
- 3 tablespoons 1% milk
- ½ teaspoon dried thyme

Easy Banger Pizza | Serves 4

- 2 tablespoons ketchup
- 1 pitta bread
- 80 g banger meat
- 230 g Cheddar cheese
- 1 teaspoon garlic powder
- 1 tablespoon rapeseed oil

Prepare for Asparagus and Pepper Strata:
1. In a baking pan, combine the asparagus, carrot, red pepper, and 1 tablespoon of water. Then, place the pan in zone 1. air fryer at 170ºC for 3 to 5 minutes, or until crisp-tender. Drain well. 2. In a medium bowl, whisk the egg whites, egg, milk, and thyme until frothy.

Prepare for Easy Banger Pizza:
1. Spread the ketchup over the pitta bread. 2. Top with the banger meat and cheese. Sprinkle with the garlic powder and rapeseed oil. 3. Put the pizza in the zone 2 air fryer basket.

Cook:
1. Select zone 1, Select BAKE, set temperature to 170ºC, set time between 3 to 5 minutes. 2. Select zone 2, Select BAKE, set temperature to 170ºC, set time to 6 minutes. 3. Press SMART COOK. 4. press START/PAUSE to begin. 5. After 3 to 5 minutes, press PAUSE button to pause the air fryer. Open the zone 1 basket and add the bread cubes to the vegetables and gently toss. Pour the egg mixture into the pan. Bake for 11 to 15 minutes, or until the strata is slightly puffy and set and the top starts to brown. Serve. 6. Reinsert the zone 1 basket in unit, select zone 1, select BAKE, set temperature to 170ºC, set time to 11-15 minutes. Then select SMART COOK. zone 2 setting may remain the same. Finally, press START/PAUSE to continue cooking.

Onion Omelette

Prep time: 10 minutes | Cook time: 12 minutes | Serves 2

- 3 eggs
- Salt and ground black pepper, to taste
- ½ teaspoons soy sauce
- 1 large onion, chopped
- 2 tablespoons grated Cheddar cheese
- Cooking spray

1. Preheat the air fryer to 180ºC. 2. In a bowl, whisk together the eggs, salt, pepper, and soy sauce. 3. Spritz a small pan with cooking spray. Spread the chopped onion across the bottom of the pan, then transfer the pan to the zone 1 air fryer. 4. Select zone 1, Select AIR FRY, set temperature to 180ºC, set time to 6 minutes. Then press START/PAUSE to begin cooking until the onion is translucent. 5. Press PAUSE button to pause the air fryer. Add the egg mixture on top of the onions to coat well. Add the cheese on top, set time to 6 minutes. Then press START/PAUSE to continue cooking. 6. Allow to cool before serving.

Vanilla Muesli

Prep time: 5 minutes | Cook time: 40 minutes | Serves 4

- 235 g porridge oats
- 3 tablespoons maple syrup
- 1 tablespoon sunflower oil
- 1 tablespoon coconut sugar
- ¼ teaspoon vanilla
- ¼ teaspoon cinnamon
- ¼ teaspoon sea salt

1. Preheat the air fryer to 120ºC. 2. Mix together the oats, maple syrup, sunflower oil, coconut sugar, vanilla, cinnamon, and sea salt in a medium bowl and stir to combine. Transfer the mixture to a baking pan. 3. Place the pan in the air fryer baskets. Select zone 1, select BAKE, set temperature to 120ºC, and set time to 40 minutes. 4. Select MATCH COOK to match zone 2 settings to zone 1. Press the START/PAUSE button to begin cooking. Stir the muesli four times during cooking. 5. Let the muesli stand for 5 to 10 minutes before serving.

Tomato and Cheddar Rolls

Prep time: 30 minutes | Cook time: 25 minutes | Makes 12 rolls

- 4 vine tomatoes
- ½ clove garlic, minced
- 1 tablespoon rapeseed oil
- ¼ teaspoon dried thyme
- Salt and freshly ground black pepper, to taste
- 500 g plain flour
- 1 teaspoon fast-action yeast
- 2 teaspoons sugar
- 2 teaspoons salt
- 1 tablespoon rapeseed oil
- 235 g grated Cheddar cheese, plus more for sprinkling at the end
- 350 ml water

1. Cut the tomatoes in half, remove the seeds with your fingers and transfer to a bowl. Add the garlic, rapeseed oil, dried thyme, salt and freshly ground black pepper and toss well. 2. Preheat the air fryer to 200°C. 3. Place the tomatoes, cut side up in zone 1 and zone 2 air fryer baskets. Select zone 1, Select AIR FRY, set temperature to 200°C, set time to 10 minutes. Then press MATCH COOK to match zone 2 setting to zone 1. After that, press START/PAUSE to begin. The tomatoes should just start to brown. 4. Press PAUSE button to pause the air fryer. Shake the basket to redistribute the tomatoes, set the temperature down to 170°C, press START/PAUSE to bake another 5 to 10 minutes. until the tomatoes are no longer juicy. Let the tomatoes cool and then rough chop them. 5. Combine the flour, yeast, sugar and salt in the bowl of a stand mixer. Add the rapeseed oil, chopped roasted tomatoes and Cheddar cheese to the flour mixture and start to mix using the dough hook attachment. As you're mixing, add 300 ml of the water, mixing until the dough comes together. Continue to knead the dough with the dough hook for another 10 minutes, adding enough water to the dough to get it to the right consistency. 6. Transfer the dough to an oiled bowl, cover with a clean kitchen towel and let it rest and rise until it has doubled in volume, about 1 to 2 hours. Then, divide the dough into 12 equal portions. Roll each portion of dough into a ball. Lightly coat each dough ball with oil and let the dough balls rest and rise a second time, covered lightly with cling film for 45 minutes. (Alternately, you tin place the rolls in the refrigerator overnight and take them out 2 hours before you bake them.) 7. Preheat the air fryer to 180°C. 8. Spray the dough balls and the air fryer basket with a little rapeseed oil. Place the rolls in the zone 1 and zone 2 baskets. Add a little grated Cheddar cheese on top of the rolls for the last 2 minutes of air frying for an attractive finish. 9. Select zone 1, Select AIR FRY, set temperature to 180°C, set time to 10 minutes. Then press MATCH COOK to match zone 2 setting to zone 1. After that, press START/PAUSE to begin. 10. Press PAUSE button to pause the air fryer. Add a little grated Cheddar cheese on top of the rolls for the last 2 minutes of air frying for an attractive finish.

Lemon-Blueberry Muffins

Prep time: 5 minutes | Cook time: 20 to 25 minutes | Makes 6 muffins

- 150 g almond flour
- 3 tablespoons granulated sweetener
- 1 teaspoon baking powder
- 2 large eggs
- 3 tablespoons melted butter
- 1 tablespoon almond milk
- 1 tablespoon fresh lemon juice
- 120 g fresh blueberries

1. Preheat the air fryer to 180°C. Lightly coat 6 silicone muffin cups with vegetable oil. Set aside. 2. In a large mixing bowl, combine the almond flour, sweetener, and baking soda. Set aside. 3. In a separate small bowl, whisk together the eggs, butter, milk, and lemon juice. Add the egg mixture to the flour mixture and stir until just combined. Fold in the blueberries and let the batter sit for 5 minutes. 4. Spoon the muffin batter into the muffin cups, about two-thirds full. Then separate them into zone 1 and zone 2 air fryer baskets. 5. Select zone 1 and choose the BAKE. Adjust the temperature to 180°C and set the cooking time between 20 and 25 minutes. Next, press MATCH COOK to match zone 2 settings to zone 1. Once everything is set, initiate the cooking process by pressing START/PAUSE until a toothpick inserted into the center of a muffin comes out clean. 6. Remove the basket from the air fryer and let the muffins cool for about 5 minutes before transferring them to a wire rack to cool completely.

Chapter 1 Breakfasts   11

Chapter 2 Family Favorites

Chapter 2 Family Favorites

Mushroom and Green Bean Casserole

Prep time: 10 minutes | Cook time: 15 minutes | Serves 4

- 4 tablespoons unsalted butter
- 60 g diced brown onion
- 120 g chopped white mushrooms
- 120 ml double cream
- 30 g full fat soft white cheese
- 120 g chicken broth
- ¼ teaspoon xanthan gum
- 450 g fresh green beans, edges trimmed
- 14 g pork crackling, finely ground

1. In a medium skillet over medium heat, melt the butter. 2. Sauté the onion and mushrooms until they become soft and fragrant, about 3 to 5 minutes. 3. Add the double cream, soft white cheese, and broth to the pan. 4. Whisk until smooth. 5. Bring to a boil and then reduce to a simmer. 6. Sprinkle the xanthan gum into the pan and remove from heat. 7. Preheat the air fryer to 160ºC. 8. Chop the green beans into 2-inch pieces and place into a baking dish. 9. Pour the sauce mixture over them and stir until coated 10. Top the dish with minced pork crackling. 11. Separate them into zone 1 and zone 2 air fryer baskets. 12. Select zone 1, select AIR FRY, set temperature to 160ºC, set time to 15 minutes. Press MATCH COOK to match zone 2 to zone 1. Then, press START/PAUSE to begin. 13.Top will be golden and green beans fork-tender when fully cooked. 13. Serve warm.

Veggie Tuna Melts

Prep time: 15 minutes | Cook time: 7 to 11 minutes | Serves 4

- 2 low-salt wholemeal English muffins, split
- 1 (170 g) tin chunk light low-salt tuna, drained
- 235 g shredded carrot
- 80 g chopped mushrooms
- 2 spring onions, white and green parts, sliced
- 80 ml fat-free Greek yoghurt
- 2 tablespoons low-salt wholegrain mustard
- 2 slices low-salt low-fat Swiss cheese, halved

1. Place the English muffin halves in zone 1 and zone 2 air fryer baskets. 2. Select zone 1, select BAKE, set temperature 170ºC, set time to 3-4 minutes. Press MATCH COOK to match zone 2 with zone 1. Then press START/PAUSE to begin. Remove from the baskets and set aside. 3. In a medium bowl, thoroughly mix the tuna, carrot, mushrooms, spring onions, yoghurt, and mustard. 4. Top each half of the muffins with one-fourth of the tuna mixture and a half slice of Swiss cheese. 5. Reinsert the baskets into zone 1 and zone 2. Select zone 1, select BAKE, set temperature 170ºC , set time to 4-7 minutes. Press MATCH COOK to match zone 2 with zone 1. Then press START/PAUSE to begin until the tuna mixture is hot and the cheese melts and starts to brown. 6. Serve immediately.

Puffed Egg Tarts

Prep time: 10 minutes | Cook time: 42 minutes | Makes 4 tarts

- Oil, for spraying
- Plain flour, for dusting
- 1 (340 g) sheet frozen puff pastry, thawed
- 180 g shredded Cheddar cheese, divided
- 4 large eggs
- 2 teaspoons chopped fresh parsley
- Salt and ground black pepper, to taste

1. Preheat the air fryer to 200ºC. 2. Line the zone 1 and zone 2 air fryer baskets with parchment and spray lightly with oil. Lightly dust your work surface with flour. 3. Unfold the puff pastry and cut it into 4 equal squares. 4. Place 2 squares in the prepared basket. Cook for 10 minutes. 5. Remove the baskets. Press the centre of each tart shell with a spoon to make an indentation. 6. Sprinkle 3 tablespoons of cheese into each indentation and crack 1 egg into the centre of each tart shell. 7. Cook for another 7 to 11 minutes, or until the eggs are cooked to your desired doneness. 8. Select zone 1, select BAKE, set temperature to 200ºC, set time to 10 minutes. Press MATCH COOK to match zone 2 with zone 1. Then, press START/PAUSE to begin. After 10 minutes, take the baskets out from zone 1 AND zone 2, do the rest steps from the recipe. Then, set time to 7-11 minutes, reinsert the baskets into the units. Finally, press START/PAUSE to continue. 9. Sprinkle evenly with the parsley, and season with salt and black pepper. 10. Serve immediately.

Meatball Subs

Prep time: 15 minutes | Cook time: 19 minutes | Serves 6

- Oil, for spraying
- 450 g 15% fat minced beef
- 120 ml Italian breadcrumbs (mixed breadcrumbs, Italian seasoning and salt)
- 1 tablespoon dried minced onion
- 1 tablespoon minced garlic
- 1 large egg
- 1 teaspoon salt
- 1 teaspoon freshly ground black pepper
- 6 sub rolls
- 1 (510 g) jar marinara sauce
- 350 ml shredded Mozzarella cheese

1. Line the zone 1 and zone 2 air fryer baskets with parchment and spray lightly with oil. 2. In a large bowl, mix together the ground beef, bread crumbs, onion, garlic, egg, salt, and black pepper. Roll the mixture into 18 meatballs. 3. Place the meatballs in the prepared zone 1 and zone 2 baskets. 4. SELECT zone 1, select AIR FRY, set temperature to 200ºC, set time to 15 minutes. Press MATCH COOK to match zone 2 with zone 1. Then press START/PAUSE to begin. 5. Place 3 meatballs in each hoagie roll. Top with marinara and Mozzarella cheese. 6. Place the loaded rolls in the zone 1 and zone 2 air fryers. 7. Select zone 1, set time to 3-4 minutes. Press MATCH COOK to match zone 2 with zone 1. Then press START/PAUSE to complete until the cheese is melted. 8. Serve immediately.

Apple Pie Egg Rolls

Prep time: 10 minutes | Cook time: 8 minutes | Makes 6 rolls

- Oil, for spraying
- 1 (600 g) tin apple pie filling
- 1 tablespoon plain flour
- ½ teaspoon lemon juice
- ¼ teaspoon ground nutmeg
- ¼ teaspoon ground cinnamon
- 6 egg roll wrappers

1. Preheat the air fryer to 200ºC. 2. Line the zone 1 and zone 2 air fryer baskets with parchment and spray lightly with oil. 3. In a medium bowl, mix together the pie filling, flour, lemon juice, nutmeg, and cinnamon. 4. Lay out the egg roll wrappers on a work surface and spoon a dollop of pie filling in the centre of each. 5. Fill a small bowl with water. Dip your finger in the water and, working one at a time, moisten the edges of the wrappers. 6. Fold the wrapper like a packet: First fold one corner into the centre. 7. Fold each side corner in, and then fold over the remaining corner, making sure each corner overlaps a bit and the moistened edges stay closed. 8. Use additional water and your fingers to seal any open edges. 9. Place the rolls in the prepared zone 1 and zone 2 baskets and spray liberally with oil. 10. Select zone 1, Select BAKE, set temperature to 200ºC, set time to 4 minutes. Then press MATCH COOK to match zone 2 with zone 1. After that, press START/PAUSE to begin. 11. 4 minutes later, press PAUSE button to pause the air fryer. Flip, spray with oil, reinsert the baskets into zone 1 and zone 2. Then, set time to 4 minutes, press MATCH COOK to match zone 2 with zone 1. Finally, press START/PAUSE to continue or until crispy and golden brown. 12. Serve immediately.

Avocado and Egg Burrito

Prep time: 10 minutes | Cook time: 3 to 5 minutes | Serves 4

- 2 hard-boiled egg whites, chopped
- 1 hard-boiled egg, chopped
- 1 avocado, peeled, pitted, and chopped
- 1 red pepper, chopped
- 3 tablespoons low-salt salsa, plus additional for serving (optional)
- 1 (34 g) slice low-salt, low-fat processed cheese, torn into pieces
- 4 low-salt wholemeal flour wraps

1. In a medium bowl, thoroughly mix the egg whites, egg, avocado, red pepper, salsa, and cheese. 2. Place the maize wraps on a work surface and evenly divide the filling among them. 3. Fold in the edges and roll up. Secure the burritos with toothpicks if necessary. 4. Put the burritos in zone 1 and zone 2 air fryer baskets. 5. Select zone 1, select BAKE, set temperature to 200ºC, set time to 3-5 minutes. Then press MATCH COOK to match zone 2 with zone 1. Finally, press START/PAUSE to begin until the burritos are light golden brown and crisp. 6. Serve with more salsa (if using).

Meringue Cookies

Prep time: 15 minutes | Cook time: 1 hour 30 minutes | Makes 20 cookies

- Oil, for spraying
- 4 large egg whites
- 185 g sugar
- Pinch cream of tartar

1. Preheat the air fryer to 60ºC. 2. Line the zone 1 and zone 2 air fryer baskets with parchment and spray lightly with oil. 3. In a small heatproof bowl, whisk together the egg whites and sugar. 4. Fill a small saucepan halfway with water, place it over medium heat, and bring to a light simmer. 5. Place the bowl with the egg whites on the saucepan, making sure the bottom of the bowl does not touch the water. 6. Whisk the mixture until the sugar is dissolved. Transfer the mixture to a large bowl and add the cream of tartar. 7. Using an electric mixer, beat the mixture on high until it is glossy and stiff peaks form. 8. Transfer the mixture to a piping bag or a zip-top plastic bag with a corner cut off. Pipe rounds into the prepared basket. 9. Select zone 1, select BAKE, set temperature to 60ºC, set time to 1 hour 30 minutes. Press MATCH COOK to match zone 2 with zone 1. Finally, press START/PAUSE to begin. 10. Turn off the air fryer and let the meringues cool completely inside. 11. The residual heat will continue to dry them out.

Scallops with Green Vegetables

Prep time: 15 minutes | Cook time: 8 to 11 minutes | Serves 4

- 235 g runner beans
- 235 g garden peas
- 235 g frozen chopped broccoli
- 2 teaspoons olive oil
- ½ teaspoon dried basil
- ½ teaspoon dried oregano
- 340 g sea scallops

1. In a large bowl, toss the runner beans, peas, and broccoli with the olive oil. 2. Place in zone 1 and zone 2 air fryer baskets. 3. Select zone 1, select AIR FRY, set temperature to 200°C, set time to 4-6 minutes. Press MATCH COOK to match zone 2 to zone 1. Then, press START/PAUSE to begin until the vegetables are crisp-tender. 4. Remove the vegetables from the air fryer baskets and sprinkle with the herbs. Set aside. 5. In the two air fryer baskets, put the scallops. Select zone 1, Set time to 4-5 minutes. Press MATCH COOK. Finally, press START/PAUSE to continue cooking. until the scallops are firm and reach an internal temperature of just 64°C on a meat thermometer. 6. Toss scallops with the vegetables and serve immediately.

Personal Cauliflower Pizzas

Prep time: 10 minutes | Cook time: 25 minutes | Serves 2

- 1 (340 g) bag frozen riced cauliflower
- 75 g shredded Mozzarella cheese
- 15 g almond flour
- 20 g Parmesan cheese
- 1 large egg
- ½ teaspoon salt
- 1 teaspoon garlic powder
- 1 teaspoon dried oregano
- 4 tablespoons no-sugar-added marinara sauce, divided
- 110 g fresh Mozzarella, chopped, divided
- 140 g cooked chicken breast, chopped, divided
- 100 g chopped cherry tomatoes, divided
- 5 g fresh baby rocket, divided

1. Preheat the air fryer to 200°C. Cut 4 sheets of parchment paper to fit the zone 1 and zone 2 baskets of the air fryer. Brush with olive oil and set aside. 2. In a large glass bowl, microwave the cauliflower according to package directions. Place the cauliflower on a clean towel, draw up the sides, and squeeze tightly over a sink to remove the excess moisture. Return the cauliflower to the bowl and add the shredded Mozzarella along with the almond flour, Parmesan, egg, salt, garlic powder, and oregano. Stir until thoroughly combined. 3. Divide the dough into two equal portions. Place one piece of dough on the prepared parchment paper and pat gently into a thin, flat disk 7 to 8 inches in diameter. 4. Select zone 1, Select AIR FRY, set temperature to 200°C, set time to 15 minutes. Then press MATCH COOK to match zone 2 with zone 1. After that, press START/PAUSE to begin. until the crust begins to brown. Let cool for 5 minutes. 5. Transfer the parchment paper with the crust on top to a baking sheet. Place a second sheet of parchment paper over the crust. While holding the edges of both sheets together, carefully lift the crust off the baking sheet, flip it, and place it back in the air fryer basket. The new sheet of parchment paper is now on the bottom. Remove the top piece of paper. Select zone 1, Set time to 15 minutes, press MATCH COOK to match zone 2 with zone 1. After that, press START/PAUSE to begin until the top begins to brown. Remove the basket from the air fryer. 6. Spread 2 tablespoons of the marinara sauce on top of the crust, followed by half the fresh Mozzarella, chicken, cherry tomatoes, and rocket. 7. Select zone 1, Select AIR FRY, set time to 5-10 minutes. Then press MATCH COOK to match zone 2 with zone 1. After that, press START/PAUSE to begin until the cheese is melted and beginning to brown. Remove the pizza from the oven and let it sit for 10 minutes before serving.

Fried Green Tomatoes

Prep time: 15 minutes | Cook time: 6 to 8 minutes | Serves 4

- 4 medium green tomatoes
- 50 g plain flour
- 2 egg whites
- 60 ml almond milk
- 235 g ground almonds
- 120 g Japanese breadcrumbs
- 2 teaspoons olive oil
- 1 teaspoon paprika
- 1 clove garlic, minced

1. Rinse the tomatoes and pat dry. 2. Cut the tomatoes into ½-inch slices, discarding the thinner ends. Put the flour on a plate. 3. In a shallow bowl, beat the egg whites with the almond milk until frothy. 4. And on another plate, combine the almonds, breadcrumbs, olive oil, paprika, and garlic and mix well. 5. Dip the tomato slices into the flour, then into the egg white mixture, then into the almond mixture to coat. 6. Place the coated tomato slices in zone 1 and zone 2 air fryer baskets. 7. Select zone 1, select BAKE, set temperature to 200°, set time to 6-8 minutes. Then press MATCH COOK, match zone 2 setting to zone 1. Finally, press START/PAUSE to begin until the tomato coating is crisp and golden brown. 8. serve immediately.

Chapter 3: Fast and Easy Everyday Favourites

Chapter 3 Fast and Easy Everyday Favourites

Baked Chorizo Scotch Eggs

Prep time: 5 minutes | Cook time: 15 to 20 minutes | Makes 4 eggs

- 450 g Mexican chorizo or other seasoned banger meat
- 4 soft-boiled eggs plus 1 raw egg
- 1 tablespoon water
- 120 ml plain flour
- 235 ml panko breadcrumbs
- Cooking spray

1. Divide the chorizo into 4 equal portions. Flatten each portion into a disc. Place a soft-boiled egg in the centre of each disc. Wrap the chorizo around the egg, encasing it completely. Place the encased eggs on a plate and chill for at least 30 minutes. 2. Preheat the air fryer to 182°C. 3. Beat the raw egg with 1 tablespoon of water. Place the flour on a small plate and the panko on a second plate. Working with 1 egg at a time, roll the encased egg in the flour, then dip it in the egg mixture. Dredge the egg in the panko and place on a plate. Repeat with the remaining eggs. 4. Spray the eggs with oil and place in the zone 1 and zone 2 air fryer baskets. Select zone 1, select BAKE, set temperature to 182°C, set time to 10 minutes. Press MATCH COOK to match zone 2setting to zone 1. Then, press START/PAUSE to begin. 5. After 10 minutes, take them out from zone 1 and zone 2 air fryers, turn it over and then select zone 1, set time to 5-10 minutes. Press MATCH COOK to match zone 2 setting to zone 1. Finally, press START/PAUSE to finish cooking. Serve immediately.

Cheesy Jalapeño Cornbread

Prep time: 10 minutes | Cook time: 20 minutes | Serves 8

- 160 ml cornmeal
- 80 ml plain flour
- ¾ teaspoon baking powder
- 2 tablespoons margarine, melted
- ½ teaspoon rock salt
- 1 tablespoon granulated sugar
- 180 ml whole milk
- 1 large egg, beaten
- 1 red chilli, thinly sliced
- 80 ml shredded extra mature Cheddar cheese
- Cooking spray

1. Preheat the air fryer to 152°C. Spritz the zone 1 and zone 2 air fryer baskets with cooking spray. 2. Combine all the ingredients in a large bowl. Stir to mix well. Pour the mixture in a baking pan. 3. Arrange the pan in the preheated air fryer. Select zone 1, select BAKE, set temperature to 152°C, set time to 20 minutes. Press MATCH COOK to match zone 2 setting to zone 1. Then, press START/PAUSE to begin until a toothpick inserted in the centre of the bread comes out clean. 4. When the cooking is complete, remove the baking pan from zone 1 and zone2, and allow the bread to cool for a few minutes before slicing to serve.

Easy Devils on Horseback

Prep time: 5 minutes | Cook time: 7 minutes | Serves 12

- 24 small pitted prunes (128 g)
- 60 g crumbled blue cheese, divided
- 8 slices middle bacon, cut crosswise into thirds

1. Preheat the air fryer to 200°C. 2. Halve the prunes lengthwise, but don't cut them all the way through. 3. Place ½ teaspoon of cheese in the centre of each prune. 4. Wrap a piece of bacon around each prune and secure the bacon with a toothpick. 5. Working in batches, arrange a single layer of the prunes in the zone 1 and zone 2 air fryer baskets. 6. Select zone 1, select AIR FRY, set temperature to 200°C, set time to 7 minutes. Press MATCH COOK to match zone 2 with zone 1. Then, press START/PAUSE to begin. Flipping halfway, until the bacon is cooked through and crisp. 7. Let cool slightly and serve warm.

Beef Bratwursts

Prep time: 5 minutes | Cook time: 15 minutes | Serves 4

- 4 (85 g) beef bratwursts

1. Preheat the air fryer to 190°C. Place the beef bratwursts in the zone 1 and zone2. 2. Select zone 1, select AIR FRY, set temperature to 190°C, set time to 15 minutes. Press MATCH COOK to match zone 2 to zone 1. Then, press START/PAUSE to begin. turning once halfway through. Serve hot.

Bacon Pinwheels

Prep time: 10 minutes | Cook time: 10 minutes | Makes 8 pinwheels

- 1 sheet puff pastry
- 2 tablespoons maple syrup
- 48 g brown sugar
- 8 slices bacon
- Ground black pepper, to taste
- Cooking spray

1. Preheat the air fryer to 180°C. 2. Spritz the zone 1 and zone 2 air fryer baskets with cooking spray. 3. Roll the puff pastry into a 10-inch square with a rolling pin on a clean work surface, then cut the pastry into 8 strips. 4. Brush the strips with maple syrup and sprinkle with sugar, leaving a 1-inch far end uncovered. 5. Arrange each slice of bacon on each strip, leaving a ⅛-inch length of bacon hang over the end close to you. Sprinkle with black pepper. 6. From the end close to you, roll the strips into pinwheels, then dab the uncovered end with water and seal the rolls. 7. Arrange the pinwheels in the preheated zone 1 and zone 2 air fryer and spritz with cooking spray. 8. Select zone 1, select BAKE, set temperature to 180°C, set time to 10 minutes. Press MATCH COOK to match zone 2 with zone 1. Finally, press START/PAUSE to begin until golden brown. 9. Flip the pinwheels halfway through. 10. Serve immediately.

Purple Potato Chips with Rosemary

Prep time: 10 minutes | Cook time: 9 to 14 minutes | Serves 6

- 235 ml Greek yoghurt
- 2 chipotle chillies, minced
- 2 tablespoons adobo or chipotle sauce
- 1 teaspoon paprika
- 1 tablespoon lemon juice
- 10 purple fingerling or miniature potatoes
- 1 teaspoon olive oil
- 2 teaspoons minced fresh rosemary leaves
- ⅛ teaspoon cayenne pepper
- ¼ teaspoon coarse sea salt

1. Preheat the air fryer to 200°C. 2. In a medium bowl, combine the yoghurt, minced chillies, adobo sauce, paprika, and lemon juice. Mix well and refrigerate. 3. Wash the potatoes and dry them with paper towels. 4. Slice the potatoes lengthwise, as thinly as possible. You tin use a mandoline, a vegetable peeler, or a very sharp knife. 5. Combine the potato slices in a medium bowl and drizzle with the olive oil; toss to coat. 6. elect zone 1, select AIR FRY, set temperature to 200°C, set time to 9-14 minutes. Press MATCH COOK to match zone 2 with zone 1. Then press START/PAUSE to begin. 7. Use tongs to gently rearrange the chips halfway during cooking time. 8. Sprinkle the chips with the rosemary, cayenne pepper, and sea salt. 9. Serve with the chipotle sauce for dipping.

Air Fried Shishito Peppers

Prep time: 5 minutes | Cook time: 5 minutes | Serves 4

- 230 g shishito or Padron peppers (about 24)
- 1 tablespoon olive oil
- Coarse sea salt, to taste
- Lemon wedges, for serving
- Cooking spray

1. Preheat the air fryer to 200°C. 2. Spritz the zone 1 and zone 2 air fryer baskets with cooking spray. 3. Toss the peppers with olive oil in a large bowl to coat well. Arrange the peppers in the preheated zone 1 and zone 2 air fryer baskets. 4. Select zone 1, select AIR FRY, set temperature to 200°C, set time to 5 minutes. Press MATCH COOK to match zone 2 with zone 1. 5. Press START/PAUSE to begin until blistered and lightly charred. Shake the basket and sprinkle the peppers with salt halfway through the cooking time. 6. Transfer the peppers onto a plate and squeeze the lemon wedges on top before serving.

Peppery Brown Rice Fritters

Prep time: 10 minutes | Cook time: 8 to 10 minutes | Serves 4

- 1 (284 g) bag frozen cooked brown rice, thawed
- 1 egg
- 3 tablespoons brown rice flour
- 80 g finely grated carrots
- 80 g minced red pepper
- 2 tablespoons minced fresh basil
- 3 tablespoons grated Parmesan cheese
- 2 teaspoons olive oil

1. Preheat the air fryer to 190°C. 2. In a small bowl, combine the thawed rice, egg, and flour and mix to blend. 3. Stir in the carrots, pepper, basil, and Parmesan cheese. 4. Form the mixture into 8 fritters and drizzle with the olive oil. 5. Put the fritters carefully into the zone 1 and zone 2 air fryer baskets. 6. Select zone 1, select AIR FRY, set temperature to 190°C, set time to 8-10 minutes. Press MATCH COOK to match zone 2 with zone 1. Finally, press START/PAUSE to begin until the fritters are golden brown and cooked through. 7. Serve immediately.

Southwest Corn and Pepper Roast

Prep time: 10 minutes | Cook time: 10 minutes | Serves 4

For the Corn:
- 350 g thawed frozen corn kernels
- 235 g mixed diced peppers
- 1 jalapeño, diced
- 235 g diced brown onion
- ½ teaspoon ancho chilli powder
- 1 tablespoon fresh lemon juice
- 1 teaspoon ground cumin
- ½ teaspoon rock salt
- Cooking spray

For Serving:
- 60 g feta cheese
- 60 g chopped fresh coriander
- 1 tablespoon fresh lemon juice

1. Preheat the air fryer to 190ºC. 2. Spritz the zone 1 and zone 2 air fryer with cooking spray. 3. Combine the ingredients for the corn in a large bowl. 4. Stir to mix well. 5. Pour the mixture into the zone 1 and zone 2 air fryer. 6. Select zone 1, select AIR FRY, set temperature to 190ºC, set time to 10 minutes. Press MATCH COOK to match zone 2 with zone 1. Then, press START/PAUSE to begin until the corn and peppers are soft. 7. Shake the basket halfway through the cooking time. 8. Transfer them onto a large plate, then spread with feta cheese and coriander. 9. Drizzle with lemon juice and serve.

Chapter 3 Fast and Easy Everyday Favorites

Chapter 4: Beef, Pork, and Lamb

Chapter 4 Beef, Pork, and Lamb

Spicy Lamb Sirloin Chops & Air Fried Broccoli

Prep time: 35 minutes | Cook time: 15 minutes

Spicy Lamb Sirloin Chops | Serves 4:
- ½ brown onion, coarsely chopped
- 4 coin-size slices peeled fresh ginger
- 5 garlic cloves
- 1 teaspoon garam masala
- 1 teaspoon ground fennel
- 1 teaspoon ground cinnamon
- 1 teaspoon ground turmeric
- ½ to 1 teaspoon cayenne pepper
- ½ teaspoon ground cardamom
- 1 teaspoon coarse or flaky salt
- 450 g lamb sirloin chops

Air Fired Broccoli | Serves 1:
- 4 egg yolks
- 60 g melted butter
- 240 g coconut flour
- Salt and pepper, to taste
- 475 g broccoli florets

Prepare for Spicy Lamb Sirloin Chops:
1. In a blender, combine the onion, ginger, garlic, garam masala, fennel, cinnamon, turmeric, cayenne, cardamom, and salt. Pulse until the onion is finely minced and the mixture forms a thick paste, 3 to 4 minutes. 2. Place the lamb chops in a large bowl. Slash the meat and fat with a sharp knife several times to allow the marinade to penetrate better. Add the spice paste to the bowl and toss the lamb to coat. Marinate at room temperature for 30 minutes or cover and refrigerate for up to 24 hours. 3. Place the lamb chops in a single layer in the zone 1 air fryer basket.

Prepare for Air Fired Broccoli:
1. Preheat the air fryer to 200ºC. In a bowl, whisk the egg yolks and melted butter together. 2. Throw in the coconut flour, salt and pepper, then stir again to combine well. 3. Dip each broccoli floret into the mixture and place in the zone 2 air fryer basket.

Cook:
1. Select zone 1, select ROAST, set temperature to 160ºC, set time to 15 minutes. 2. Select zone 2, select AIR FRY, set temperature to 200ºC, set time to 6 minutes. 3. press SMART COOK. Press START/PAUSE to begin cooking. 4. In zone 1, turning the chops halfway through the cooking time. Use a meat thermometer to ensure the lamb has reached an internal temperature of 64ºC (medium-rare). 5. Take care when removing them from the air fryer and serve immediately.

Chorizo and Beef Burger

Prep time: 10 minutes | Cook time: 15 minutes | Serves 4

- 340 g 80/20 beef mince
- 110 g Mexican-style chorizo crumb
- 60 g chopped onion
- 5 slices pickled jalapeños, chopped
- 2 teaspoons chilli powder
- 1 teaspoon minced garlic
- ¼ teaspoon cumin

1. In a large bowl, mix all ingredients. Divide the mixture into four sections and form them into burger patties. 2. Place burger patties into the zone 1 and zone 2 air fryer basket. 3. Select zone 1, select ROAST, set temperature to 190ºC, set time to 15 minutes. Press MATCH COOK to match zone 2 to zone 1. Then, press START/PAUSE to begin. 4. Flip the patties halfway through the cooking time. 5. Serve warm.

Bacon-Wrapped Hot Dogs with Mayo-Ketchup Sauce

Prep time: 5 minutes | Cook time: 10 to 12 minutes | Serves 5

- 10 thin slices of bacon
- 5 pork hot dogs, halved

Sauce:
- 60 ml mayonnaise
- 4 tablespoons ketchup
- 1 teaspoon cayenne pepper
- 1 teaspoon rice vinegar
- 1 teaspoon chilli powder

1. Preheat the air fryer to 200ºC. 2. Arrange the slices of bacon on a clean work surface. One by one, place the halved hot dog on one end of each slice, season with cayenne pepper and wrap the hot dog with the bacon slices and secure with toothpicks as needed. 3. place the wrapped hot dogs in the zone 1 and zone 2 air fryer baskets. Select zone 1, select ROAST, set temperature 200ºC, set time to 10-12 minutes. Press MATCH COOK to match zone 2 setting to zone 1. Then, press START/PAUSE to begin until the bacon becomes browned and crispy. 4. Make the sauce: Stir all the ingredients for the sauce in a small bowl. Wrap the bowl in plastic and set in the refrigerator until ready to serve. 5. Transfer the hot dogs to a platter and serve hot with the sauce.

Cheesy Low-Carb Lasagna & Kielbasa and Cabbage

Prep time: 20 minutes | Cook time: 20 to 25 minutes | Serves 4

Cheesy Low-Carb Lasagna | Serves 4
Meat Layer:
- Extra-virgin olive oil
- 450 g 85% lean beef mince
- 235 ml marinara sauce
- 60 g diced celery
- 60 g diced red onion
- ½ teaspoon minced garlic
- Coarse or flaky salt and black pepper, to taste

Cheese Layer:
- 230 g ricotta cheese
- 235 g shredded Mozzarella cheese
- 120 g grated Parmesan cheese
- 2 large eggs
- 1 teaspoon dried Italian seasoning, crushed
- ½ teaspoon each minced garlic, garlic powder, and black pepper

Kielbasa and Cabbage | Serves 4
- 450 g smoked kielbasa banger, sliced into ½-inch pieces
- 1 head cabbage, very coarsely chopped
- ½ brown onion, chopped
- 2 cloves garlic, chopped
- 2 tablespoons olive oil
- ½ teaspoon salt
- ½ teaspoon freshly ground black pepper
- 60 ml water

Prepare for Cheesy Low-Carb Lasagna(zone 1):
1. For the meat layer: Grease a cake pan with 1 teaspoon olive oil. 2. In a large bowl, combine the beef mince, marinara, celery, onion, garlic, salt, and pepper. Place the seasoned meat in the pan. 3. Place the pan in the zone 1 air fryer basket. 4. Meanwhile, for the cheese layer: In a medium bowl, combine the ricotta, half the Mozzarella, the Parmesan, lightly beaten eggs, Italian seasoning, minced garlic, garlic powder, and pepper. Stir until well blended. 5. At the end of the cooking time, spread the cheese mixture over the meat mixture. Sprinkle with the remaining 120 ml Mozzarella. Set the air fryer to 190ºC for 10 minutes, or until the cheese is browned and bubbling. use a meat thermometer to ensure the meat has reached an internal temperature of 72ºC. 6. Drain the fat and liquid from the pan. Let stand for 5 minutes before serving.

Prepare for Kielbasa and Cabbage(zone 2):
1. Preheat the air fryer to 200ºC. 2. In a large bowl, combine the banger, cabbage, onion, garlic, olive oil, salt, and black pepper. Toss until thoroughly combined. 3. Transfer the mixture to the zone 2 basket of the air fryer and pour the water over the top.

Cook:
1.Select zone 1, select BAKE, set temperature to 190ºC, set time to 10 minutes. 2. Select zone 2, select AIR FRY, set temperature to 200ºC, set time to 20-25 minutes. 3. Press SMART COOK. 4. Press START/PAUSE to begin. 5. For zone 2, Pausing two or three times during the cooking time to shake the basket. 6. 10 minutes later, take out the zone 1 basket, spread the cheese mixture over the meat mixture. Sprinkle with the remaining 120 ml Mozzarella. Set temperature to 190ºC, set time to 10 minutes. Then reinsert the zone 1 basket in the unit, set time to 10 minutes. 7. Press SMART COOK. Finally, START/PAUSE to finish the dishes. You may get the two dishes in the same time.

Nigerian Peanut-Crusted Bavette Steak

Prep time: 30 minutes | Cook time: 8 minutes | Serves 4

Suya Spice Mix:
- 60 g dry-roasted peanuts
- 1 teaspoon cumin seeds
- 1 teaspoon garlic powder
- 1 teaspoon smoked paprika
- ½ teaspoon ground ginger
- 1 teaspoon coarse or flaky salt
- ½ teaspoon cayenne pepper

Steak:
- 450 g bavette or skirt steak
- 2 tablespoons vegetable oil

1.In a clean coffee grinder or spice mill, combine peanuts and cumin seeds. Process them into a coarse powder, taking care not to overprocess, which could result in peanut butter. Alternatively, you can grind the cumin seeds with 80g of ready-made peanut powder instead of whole peanuts. 2. Transfer the peanut-cumin mixture to a small bowl. Add garlic powder, paprika, ground ginger, salt, and cayenne pepper. Stir the ingredients well to combine. This should yield about 120ml of suya spice mix. Store any leftover spice mix in an airtight container in a cool, dry place for up to 1 month. 3. Cut the steak against the grain into ½-inch-thick slices, at a slight angle for better tenderness. Place the beef slices in a resealable plastic bag, add oil, and then add 2½ to 3 tablespoons of the suya spice mix. Seal the bag, and massage the contents to ensure the meat is evenly coated with the oil and spice mixture. Marinate the meat at room temperature for 30 minutes or refrigerate for up to 24 hours for deeper flavor penetration. 4. Arrange the marinated beef strips in the air fryer baskets, distributing them between zone 1 and zone 2 for even cooking. Set the air fryer temperature to 200ºC and cook for 8 minutes, turning the strips halfway through to ensure even browning and crisping. 5. Select zone 1 and choose the 'Roast' function. Set the temperature to 200ºC and the timer to 8 minutes. Press the 'Match Cook' button to synchronize zone 2 with zone 1's settings. Finally, press 'Start/Pause' to begin the cooking process. 6. Once cooked, transfer the beef strips to a serving platter. If desired, sprinkle with additional suya spice mix for extra flavor and aroma. 7. Serve the spice-crusted steak with your favorite side dishes, such as a fresh salad, roasted vegetables, or mashed potatoes. The steak's exterior should be crispy from the suya spice mix, while the inside remains tender and juicy.

Bone-in Pork Chops

Prep time: 5 minutes | Cook time: 10 to 12 minutes | Serves 2

- 450 g bone-in pork chops
- 1 tablespoon avocado oil
- 1 teaspoon smoked paprika
- ½ teaspoon onion granules
- ¼ teaspoon cayenne pepper
- Sea salt and freshly ground black pepper, to taste

1. Brush both sides of the pork chops with avocado oil. In a small dish, mix together the smoked paprika, onion granules, cayenne pepper, salt, and black pepper. Sprinkle this seasoning mixture evenly over both sides of the pork chops. 2. Preheat your Ninja Dual zone Air Fryer to 200ºC (392ºF). 3. Place the seasoned pork chops in a single layer in both zone 1 and zone 2 air fryer baskets. 4. Select zone 1, choose the "ROAST" function, set the temperature to 200ºC (392ºF), and the time to 10-12 minutes. Press MATCH COOK to synchronize the settings for zone 2 with zone 1. Press START/PAUSE to begin cooking. 5. Air fry for 10-12 minutes, or until an instant-read thermometer inserted into the thickest part of the pork chops reads 64ºC (147ºF). 6. Remove the pork chops from the air fryer and let them rest for 5 minutes before serving to allow the juices to redistribute.

Asian Glazed Meatballs

Prep time: 15 minutes | Cook time: 10 minutes per batch | Serves 4 to 6

- 1 large shallot, finely chopped
- 2 cloves garlic, minced
- 1 tablespoon grated fresh ginger
- 2 teaspoons fresh thyme, finely chopped
- 355 g brown mushrooms, very finely chopped (a food processor works well here)
- 2 tablespoons soy sauce
- Freshly ground black pepper, to taste
- 450 g beef mince
- 230 g pork mince
- 3 egg yolks
- 235 ml Thai sweet chilli sauce (spring roll sauce)
- 60 g toasted sesame seeds
- 2 spring onionspring onions, sliced

1. Combine the shallot, garlic, ginger, thyme, mushrooms, soy sauce, freshly ground black pepper, beef and pork mince, and egg yolks in a bowl and mix the ingredients together. Gently shape the mixture into 24 balls, about the size of a golf ball. 2. Preheat the air fryer to 190ºC. 3. Put time into zone 1 and zone 2 baskets, air fry the meatballs for 8 minutes, turning the meatballs over halfway through the cooking time. Drizzle some of the Thai sweet chilli sauce on top of each meatball and return the basket to the air fryer, air frying for another 2 minutes. Reserve the remaining Thai sweet chilli sauce for serving. 4. As soon as the meatballs are done, sprinkle with toasted sesame seeds and transfer them to a serving platter. Scatter the spring onionspring onions around and serve warm. 5. Select zone 1, select ROAST, set temperature to 190ºC, set time to 8 minutes. Then press MATCH COOK to match zone 2 with zone 1. After that, press START/PAUSE to begin. After 8 minutes, take out zone 1 and zone 2 baskets from the air fryer, follow the recipe to finish the next steps. Then reinsert the two baskets, set time to 2 minutes, and then, press MATCH COOK. After all, press START/PAUSE to complete the dishes.

Pork Schnitzels with Sour Cream and Dill Sauce

Prep time: 5 minutes | Cook time: 24 minutes | Serves 4 to 6

- 60 g flour
- 1½ teaspoons salt
- Freshly ground black pepper, to taste
- 2 eggs
- 120 ml milk
- 180 g toasted breadcrumbs
- 1 teaspoon paprika
- 6 boneless pork chops (about 680 g), fat trimmed, pound to ½-inch thick
- 2 tablespoons olive oil
- 3 tablespoons melted butter
- Lemon wedges, for serving
- Sour Cream and Dill Sauce:
- 235 g chicken stock
- 1½ tablespoons cornflour
- 80 ml sour cream
- 1½ tablespoons chopped fresh dill
- Salt and ground black pepper, to taste

1. Preheat your Ninja Dual zone Air Fryer to 200ºC (392ºF) for both zone 1 and zone 2. 2. In a large bowl, combine the flour with salt and black pepper. Stir to mix well. In a second bowl, whisk together the egg and milk. In a third bowl, stir together the breadcrumbs and paprika. 3. Dredge each pork chop first in the flour mixture, then in the egg mixture, and finally in the breadcrumb mixture. Press to coat well and shake off any excess. 4. Place the coated pork chops in the preheated zone 1 and zone 2 air fryer baskets. Brush each pork chop with a mixture of olive oil and melted butter on all sides. 5. Select zone 1, choose the "AIR FRY" function, set the temperature to 200ºC (392ºF), and the time to 4 minutes. Press MATCH COOK to sync the settings for zone 2 with zone 1. Press START/PAUSE to begin cooking. After 4 minutes, flip the pork chops and continue air frying for another 4 minutes, or until golden brown and crispy. 6. Meanwhile, in a small saucepan, combine the chicken stock and cornflour. Bring to a boil over medium-high heat, then simmer for 2 more minutes until thickened. Turn off the heat and mix in the sour cream, fresh dill, salt, and black pepper. 7. Remove the schnitzels from the air fryer and transfer to a plate. Drizzle with the creamy dill sauce and squeeze lemon wedges over the top before serving.

Teriyaki Rump Steak with Broccoli and Capsicum

Prep time: 5 minutes | Cook time: 13 minutes | Serves 4

- 230 g rump steak
- 80 ml teriyaki marinade
- 1½ teaspoons sesame oil
- ½ head broccoli, cut into florets
- 2 red peppers, sliced
- Fine sea salt and ground black pepper, to taste
- Cooking spray

1. Preheat your Ninja Dual zone Air Fryer to 200°C (392°F) for both zone 1 and zone 2. 2. In a large bowl, combine the flour with salt and black pepper. Stir to mix well. In a second bowl, whisk together the egg and milk. In a third bowl, stir together the breadcrumbs and paprika. 3. Dredge each pork chop first in the flour mixture, then in the egg mixture, and finally in the breadcrumb mixture. Press to coat well and shake off any excess. 4. Place the coated pork chops in the preheated zone 1 and zone 2 air fryer baskets. Brush each pork chop with a mixture of olive oil and melted butter on all sides. 5. Select zone 1, choose the "AIR FRY" function, set the temperature to 200°C (392°F), and the time to 4 minutes. Press MATCH COOK to sync the settings for zone 2 with zone 1. Press START/PAUSE to begin cooking. After 4 minutes, flip the pork chops and continue air frying for another 4 minutes, or until golden brown and crispy. 6. Meanwhile, in a small saucepan, combine the chicken stock and cornflour. Bring to a boil over medium-high heat, then simmer for 2 more minutes until thickened. Turn off the heat and mix in the sour cream, fresh dill, salt, and black pepper. 7. Remove the schnitzels from the air fryer and transfer to a plate. Drizzle with the creamy dill sauce and squeeze lemon wedges over the top before serving.

Almond and Caraway Crust Steak

Prep time: 16 minutes | Cook time: 10 minutes | Serves 4

- 40 g almond flour
- 2 eggs
- 2 teaspoons caraway seeds
- 4 beef steaks
- 2 teaspoons garlic powder
- 1 tablespoon melted butter
- Fine sea salt and cayenne pepper, to taste

1. Begin by generously coating each steak with a blend of garlic powder, caraway seeds, salt, and a dash of cayenne pepper. Ensure the spices adhere well to the steak's surface. 2. In one mixing bowl, combine melted butter with seasoned bread crumbs until they are thoroughly mixed together. In a separate bowl, whisk the eggs until they are well beaten and smooth. 3. Dip each spiced steak into the beaten egg, ensuring it is fully coated. Next, press the steak into the buttered crumb mixture, evenly covering it with the crumbs. 4. Arrange the coated steaks in the air fryer basket designated for zone 1. Set the air fryer to cook at 180°C for a duration of 10 minutes. 5. Select zone 1 on your air fryer, choose the 'Roast' function, set the temperature to 180°C, and set the timer for 10 minutes. Press the 'Start/Pause' button to initiate the cooking cycle. 6. Once the timer has counted down and the steaks are cooked to a golden brown, crispy exterior, remove them from the air fryer. Allow the steaks to rest for a few minutes to ensure the juices settle before serving.

Honey-Baked Pork Loin

Prep time: 30 minutes | Cook time: 22 to 25 minutes | Serves 6

- 60 ml honey
- 60 g freshly squeezed lemon juice
- 2 tablespoons soy sauce
- 1 teaspoon garlic powder
- 1 (900 g) pork loin
- 2 tablespoons vegetable oil

1. In a medium bowl, combine honey, lemon juice, soy sauce, and garlic powder. Whisk until the ingredients are well mixed. Set aside half of this mixture to be used for basting during the cooking process. 2. Cut the pork loin into two equal pieces to ensure even cooking. Make 5 slits in each piece of pork loin to help the marinade penetrate the meat. Transfer the pork to a resealable plastic bag. 3. Pour the remaining half of the honey mixture into the bag with the pork. Seal the bag, ensuring all the pork pieces are well coated with the marinade. 4. Refrigerate the pork to marinate for at least 2 hours. A longer marination time will allow for deeper flavor penetration, up to 24 hours is recommended for the best results. 5. Set the air fryer to preheat at 200°C. While the air fryer is preheating, line the air fryer baskets for both zone 1 and zone 2 with parchment paper to prevent sticking and make clean-up easier. 6. Remove the pork from the marinade, allowing excess to drip off, and place it on the lined parchment in the air fryer baskets. Lightly spritz the surface of the pork with oil and baste with the reserved marinade. 7. Select zone 1 and choose the 'Roast' function. Set the temperature to 200°C and the timer to 15 minutes. Press the 'Match Cook' button to synchronize zone 2 with zone 1's settings. Press 'Start/Pause' to begin cooking. 8. After 15 minutes, remove the baskets from the air fryer. Flip the pork pieces, baste with more of the reserved marinade, and spritz with oil again. Reinsert the baskets into their respective zones, set the timer for an additional 7-10 minutes, and press 'Start/Pause' to continue cooking. 9. Once the cooking time has elapsed, allow the pork to rest for 5 minutes before serving. This resting period helps the juices to redistribute within the meat, resulting in a more tender and juicy pork loin. 10. After the resting time, the honey-garlic pork loin is ready to be served. Enjoy it with your favorite side dishes or as part of a larger meal.

Chapter 4 Beef, Pork, and Lamb

Mediterranean Beef Steaks

Prep time: 20 minutes | Cook time: 20 minutes | Serves 4

- 2 tablespoons soy sauce or tamari
- 3 heaping tablespoons fresh chives
- 2 tablespoons olive oil
- 3 tablespoons dry white wine
- 4 small-sized beef steaks
- 2 teaspoons smoked cayenne pepper
- ½ teaspoon dried basil
- ½ teaspoon dried rosemary
- 1 teaspoon freshly ground black pepper
- 1 teaspoon sea salt, or more to taste

1. Coat both sides of the steaks evenly with cayenne pepper, black pepper, salt, dried basil, and dried rosemary. 2. Drizzle the steaks with olive oil, white wine, and soy sauce, ensuring they are well-coated. 3. Preheat your Ninja Dual zone Air Fryer to 170°C (338°F). 4. Place the seasoned steaks in the zone 1 air fryer basket. Select zone 1, choose the "ROAST" function, set the temperature to 170°C (338°F), and the time to 20 minutes. Press START/PAUSE to begin cooking. 5. Once cooked, remove the steaks from the air fryer and let them rest for a few minutes. Garnish with freshly chopped chives before serving.

Bacon-Wrapped Pork Tenderloin

Prep time: 30 minutes | Cook time: 22 to 25 minutes | Serves 6

- 120 g minced onion
- 120 ml apple cider, or apple juice
- 60 ml honey
- 1 tablespoon minced garlic
- ¼ teaspoon salt
- ¼ teaspoon freshly ground black pepper
- 900 g pork tenderloin
- 1 to 2 tablespoons oil
- 8 uncooked bacon slices

1. In a medium-sized bowl, combine the onion, apple cider, honey, minced garlic, salt, and pepper to form a marinade. Transfer this mixture into a large resealable plastic bag or airtight container, and add the pork loin to it. Seal the bag, ensuring the pork is well-coated with the marinade. Refrigerate and allow the pork to marinate for a minimum of 2 hours to infuse the flavors. 2. Preheat both the zone 1 and zone 2 compartments of the air fryer to 200°C. Line the air fryer baskets with parchment paper to prevent sticking and ease clean-up. Remove the pork from the marinade, allowing excess to drip off, and place it on the prepared parchment paper within the air fryer baskets. Lightly spritz the surface of the pork with oil to enhance browning. 3. Select zone 1 and choose the 'Roast' function, setting the temperature to 200°C and the timer for 15 minutes. Press the 'Match Cook' button to synchronize zone 2 with zone 1's settings. Finally, press 'Start/Pause' to commence the cooking process. 4. After 15 minutes, carefully remove both zone 1 and zone 2 baskets from the air fryer. Wrap the slices of bacon around the roasted pork, securing them in place with toothpicks. Turn the pork to ensure even cooking and spritz with oil again. Reinsert the baskets into their respective zones, reset the timer for an additional 7-10 minutes, and press 'Start/Pause' to continue cooking. Monitor the internal temperature of the pork loin until it reaches 64°C, which is a safe and desirable level of doneness. Remember that the pork will continue to cook slightly as it rests, so allow it to sit for 5 minutes before carving and serving. 5. Once the pork loin has reached the desired internal temperature and rested, it is ready to be served. Slice against the grain for a tender and juicy result. Enjoy your flavorful and crispy air-fried pork loin with bacon wrapping as a delicious main course.

Ham with Sweet Potatoes

Prep time: 20 minutes | Cook time: 15 to 17 minutes | Serves 4

- 235 g freshly squeezed orange juice
- 96 g packed light brown sugar
- 1 tablespoon Dijon mustard
- ½ teaspoon salt
- ½ teaspoon freshly ground black pepper
- 3 sweet potatoes, cut into small wedges
- 2 gammon steaks (230 g each), halved
- 1 to 2 tablespoons oil

1. In a large bowl, whisk together the orange juice, brown sugar, Dijon mustard, salt, and black pepper until well blended. Add the sweet potato wedges to the bowl and toss to coat them evenly with the brown sugar mixture. Set aside. 2. Preheat your Ninja Dual zone Air Fryer to 200°C (400°F). Line the zone 1 air fryer basket with parchment paper and lightly spritz with oil. 3. Place the sweet potato wedges in the lined zone 1 basket. Select zone 1, choose the "BAKE" function, set the temperature to 200°C (400°F), and set the time to 12-14 minutes. Press START/PAUSE to begin cooking. 4. After the sweet potatoes have been cooking for 10 minutes, place the gammon steaks in the zone 2 air fryer basket. Brush the gammon steaks and the sweet potatoes with more of the orange juice mixture. 5. Select zone 2, choose the "ROAST" function, set the temperature to 200°C (400°F), and set the time to 3 minutes. Press SMART FINISH and then START/PAUSE to begin cooking. 6. After 3 minutes, pause the air fryer, remove the zone 2 basket, and flip the gammon steaks. Reinsert the basket into zone 2. Set the time to an additional 2-4 minutes and press START/PAUSE to finish cooking. 7. Once the cooking is complete, remove both the zone 1 and zone 2 baskets. Arrange the sweet potato wedges and gammon steaks on a serving platter.

Cheddar Bacon Burst with Spinach

Prep time: 5 minutes | Cook time: 60 minutes | Serves 8

- 30 slices bacon
- 1 tablespoon Chipotle chilli powder
- 2 teaspoons Italian seasoning
- 120 g Cheddar cheese
- 1 kg raw spinach

1. Preheat the air fryer to 190ºC. 2. Weave the bacon into 15 vertical pieces and 12 horizontal pieces. Cut the extra 3 in half to fill in the rest, horizontally. 3. Season the bacon with Chipotle chilli powder and Italian seasoning. 4. Add the cheese to the bacon. 5. Add the spinach and press down to compress. 6. Tightly roll up the woven bacon. 7. Line the zone 1 baking sheet with kitchen foil and add plenty of salt to it. 8. Put the bacon on top of a cooling rack and put that on top of the baking sheet. 9. Select zone 1, choose the "ROAST" function, set the temperature to 190ºC (374ºF), and set the time to 60 minutes. Press START/PAUSE to begin cooking. 10. Let cool for 15 minutes before slicing and serving.

Lamb Burger with Feta and Olives

Prep time: 10 minutes | Cook time: 20 minutes | Serves 3 to 4

- 2 teaspoons olive oil
- ⅓ onion, finely chopped
- 1 clove garlic, minced
- 450 g lamb mince
- 2 tablespoons fresh parsley, finely chopped
- 1½ teaspoons fresh oregano, finely chopped
- 120 g black olives, finely chopped
- 80 g crumbled feta cheese
- ½ teaspoon salt
- Freshly ground black pepper, to taste
- 4 thick pitta breads

1. Preheat a medium frying pan over medium-high heat on the stovetop. Add the olive oil and cook the onion until tender, but not browned, about 4 to 5 minutes. Add the garlic and cook for another minute. Transfer the onion and garlic to a mixing bowl and add the lamb mince, parsley, oregano, olives, feta cheese, salt and pepper. Gently mix the ingredients together. 2. Divide the mixture into 3 or 4 equal portions and then form the hamburgers, being careful not to over-handle the meat. One good way to do this is to throw the meat back and forth between your hands like a baseball, packing the meat each time you catch it. Flatten the balls into patties, making an indentation in the center of each patty. Flatten the sides of the patties as well to make it easier to fit them into the zone 1 and zone 2 air fryer baskets. 3. Preheat the air fryer to 190ºC. 4. Select zone 1, Select ROAST, set time to 8 minutes, set temperature to 190ºC. Press MATCH COOK to match zone 2 setting to zone 1. Then, Press START/PAUSE to begin. 5. After 8 minutes, Flip the burgers over and air fry for another 8 minutes. This should give you a medium-well burger. If you'd prefer a medium-rare burger, shorten the cooking time to about 13 minutes. Remove the burgers to a resting plate and let the burgers rest for a few minutes before dressing and serving. 6. While the burgers are resting, toast the pitta breads in the air fryer for 2 minutes. Tuck the burgers into the toasted pitta breads, or wrap the pittas around the burgers and serve with a tzatziki sauce or some mayonnaise.

Herbed Lamb Steaks

Prep time: 30 minutes | Cook time: 15 minutes | Serves 4

- ½ medium onion
- 2 tablespoons minced garlic
- 2 teaspoons ground ginger
- 1 teaspoon ground cinnamon
- 1 teaspoon onion granules
- 1 teaspoon cayenne pepper
- 1 teaspoon salt
- 4 (170 g) boneless lamb sirloin steaks
- Oil, for spraying

1. Prepare the Marinade: In a blender, combine chopped onion, garlic cloves, fresh ginger, a cinnamon stick, onion granules, cayenne pepper, and salt. Pulse the mixture until the onion is minced and the ingredients are well combined, forming a marinade. 2. Marinate the Lamb: Place the lamb steaks in a large bowl or a zip-top plastic bag. Sprinkle the onion mixture over the steaks and turn them to ensure they are evenly coated with the marinade. If using a bag, remove as much air as possible before sealing. Cover with cling film or seal the bag and refrigerate for 30 minutes to allow the flavors to penetrate the meat. 3. Preheat the Air Fryer: Set the air fryer to preheat at 160ºC. While the air fryer is preheating, line the air fryer baskets for both zone 1 and zone 2 with parchment paper and lightly spray them with oil to prevent sticking. 4. Cook the Lamb: Place the marinated lamb steaks in a single layer in the prepared air fryer baskets, ensuring that they do not overlap. This will allow for even cooking. 5. Set the Air Fryer: Select zone 1 and choose the 'Roast' function. Set the temperature to 160ºC and the timer to 8 minutes. Press the 'Match Cook' button to synchronize zone 2 with zone 1's settings. Press 'Start/Pause' to begin cooking. 6. Finish Cooking: After the initial 8 minutes, remove the baskets from the air fryer. Flip the lamb steaks and reinsert the baskets into the air fryer units. Set the timer for an additional 7 minutes. Press 'Start/Pause' to continue cooking until the lamb is cooked to your desired doneness. 7. Serve: Once the lamb steaks are cooked, remove them from the air fryer and allow them to rest for a few minutes before serving. This will help the juices to settle, resulting in a more tender and flavorful dish.

Cheese Crusted Chops

Prep time: 10 minutes | Cook time: 12 minutes | Serves 4 to 6

- ¼ teaspoon pepper
- ½ teaspoons salt
- 4 to 6 thick boneless pork chops
- 235 g pork scratching crumbs
- ¼ teaspoon chilli powder
- ½ teaspoons onion granules
- 1 teaspoon smoked paprika
- 2 beaten eggs
- 3 tablespoons grated Parmesan cheese
- Cooking spray

1. Preheat the air fryer to 210ºC. 2. Rub the pepper and salt on both sides of pork chops. 3. In a food processor, pulse pork scratchings into crumbs. Mix crumbs with chilli powder, onion granules, and paprika in a bowl. 4. Beat eggs in another bowl. 5. Dip pork chops into eggs then into pork scratchings crumb mixture. 6. Spritz the zone 1 and zone 2 air fryer basket with cooking spray and add pork chops to the basket. 7. Select zone 1, select ROAST, set temperature to 210ºC, set time to 12 minutes. Press MATCH BUTTON to match zone 2 setting to zone 1. Then, press START/PAUSE to begin. 8. Serve garnished with the Parmesan cheese.

Herb-Crusted Lamb Chops

Prep time: 10 minutes | Cook time: 5 minutes | Serves 2

- 1 large egg
- 2 cloves garlic, minced
- 60 g finely crushed pork scratchings
- 60 g pre-grated Parmesan cheese
- 1 tablespoon chopped fresh oregano leaves
- 1 tablespoon chopped fresh rosemary leaves
- 1 teaspoon chopped fresh thyme leaves
- ½ teaspoon ground black pepper
- 4 (1-inch-thick) lamb chops
- For Garnish/Serving (Optional):
- Sprigs of fresh oregano
- Sprigs of fresh rosemary
- Sprigs of fresh thyme
- Lavender flowers
- Lemon slices

1. Prepare the Air Fryer: Spray the air fryer basket with a light layer of avocado oil to prevent sticking. Preheat the air fryer to 200ºC. 2. Mix the Egg and Garlic: In a shallow bowl, beat the egg and add minced garlic. Stir well to combine, creating a garlic-infused egg wash. 3. Combine the Coating Ingredients: In another shallow bowl, mix together crushed pork scratching, grated Parmesan, chopped fresh herbs, and black pepper to create a coating mixture. 4. Coat the Lamb Chops: Dip each lamb chop one at a time into the egg mixture, allowing any excess to drip off. Then, dredge the chops in the Parmesan mixture, pressing firmly to create an even and well-adhered crust. If necessary, repeat the dipping process to ensure a thick coating. 5. Cook the Lamb Chops: Place the coated lamb chops in the air fryer baskets, ensuring there is space between each chop. Cook for 5 minutes or until the internal temperature of the meat reaches 64ºC for medium doneness. 6. Set the Air Fryer: Select zone 1 and choose the 'Roast' function. Set the temperature to 200ºC and the timer to 5 minutes. Press 'Match Cook' to synchronize zone 2 with zone 1's settings. Press 'Start/Pause' to begin cooking. 7. Rest and Serve: Allow the cooked lamb chops to rest for approximately 10 minutes before serving to let the juices redistribute. 8. Garnish and Serve: If desired, garnish the lamb chops with fresh sprigs of oregano, rosemary, and thyme, as well as lavender flowers for a touch of elegance. Accompany the dish with lemon slices for a refreshing contrast. 9. Storage and Reheating: For the best flavor and texture, serve the lamb chops fresh. Any leftovers can be stored in an airtight container in the refrigerator for up to 4 days. To reheat, place the cooled chops in a preheated 180ºC air fryer for about 3 minutes, or until heated through.

Pepper Steak

Prep time: 30 minutes | Cook time: 16 to 20 minutes | Serves 4

- 450 g minute steak, cut into 1-inch pieces
- 235 ml Italian dressing
- 355 ml beef stock
- 1 tablespoon soy sauce
- ½ teaspoon salt
- ¼ teaspoon freshly ground black pepper
- 30 g cornflour
- 235 g thinly sliced pepper, any color
- 235 g chopped celery
- 1 tablespoon minced garlic
- 1 to 2 tablespoons oil

1. In a large resealable bag, combine the beef and Italian dressing. Seal the bag and refrigerate to marinate for 8 hours. 2. In a small bowl, whisk the beef stock, soy sauce, salt, and pepper until blended. 3. In another small bowl, whisk 60 ml water and the cornflour until dissolved. Stir the cornflour mixture into the beef stock mixture until blended. 4. Preheat the air fryer to 190ºC. 5. Pour the stock mixture into zone 1 and zone 2 baking trays. Cook for 4 minutes. Select zone 1, select ROAST, set temperature to 190ºC, set time to 4 minutes. Press MATCH COOK to match zone 2 setting to zone 1. Then, press START/PAUSE to begin. After 4 minutes, press START/PAUSE to pause the air fry. Stir and cook for 4 to 5 minutes more. Remove and set aside. 6. Increase the air fryer temperature to 200ºC. Line the zone 1 and zone 2 air fryer baskets with parchment paper. 7. Remove the steak from the marinade and place it in a medium bowl. Discard the marinade. Stir in the pepper, celery, and garlic. 8. Place the steak and pepper mixture on the parchment. Spritz with oil. 9. Cook for 4 minutes. Select zone 1, select ROAST, set temperature to 200ºC, set time to 4 minutes. Press MATCH COOK to match zone 2 setting to zone 1. Then, press START/PAUSE to begin. Shake the basket and cook for 4 to 7 minutes more, until the vegetables are tender and the meat reaches an internal temperature of 64ºC. Serve with the gravy.

Bacon-Wrapped Vegetable Kebabs

Prep time: 10 minutes | Cook time: 10 to 12 minutes | Serves 4

- 110 g mushrooms, sliced
- 1 small courgette, sliced
- 12 baby plum tomatoes
- 110 g sliced bacon, halved
- Avocado oil spray
- Sea salt and freshly ground black pepper, to taste

1. Stack 3 mushroom slices, 1 courgette slice, and 1 tomato. Wrap a bacon strip around the vegetables and thread them onto a skewer. Repeat with the remaining vegetables and bacon. Spray with oil and sprinkle with salt and pepper. 2. Set the air fryer to 200ºC. Place the skewers in the zone 1 and zone 2 air fryer baskets in a single layer. 3. Selecting zone 1, select ROAST, setting the temperature to 200ºC, and setting the time to 5 minutes. Press MATCH COOK to match zone 2 setting to zone 1. Then, Select START/PAUSE to begin. 4. Flip the skewers and cook for 5 to 7 minutes more, until the bacon is crispy and the vegetables are tender. 5. Serve warm.

Vietnamese "Shaking" Beef

Prep time: 30 minutes | Cook time: 4 minutes per batch | Serves 4

Meat:
- 4 garlic cloves, minced
- 2 teaspoons soy sauce
- 2 teaspoons sugar
- 1 teaspoon toasted sesame oil

Salad:
- 2 tablespoons rice vinegar or apple cider vinegar
- 2 tablespoons vegetable oil
- 1 garlic clove, minced
- 2 teaspoons sugar
- ¼ teaspoon coarse or flaky salt
- ¼ teaspoon black pepper

For Serving:
- Lime wedges
- Coarse salt and freshly cracked black pepper, to taste

- 1 teaspoon coarse or flaky salt
- ¼ teaspoon black pepper
- 680 g flat iron or top rump steak, cut into 1-inch cubes

- ½ red onion, halved and very thinly sliced
- 1 head butterhead lettuce, leaves separated and torn into large pieces
- 120 g halved baby plum tomatoes
- 60 g fresh mint leaves

1. In a small bowl, mix together minced garlic, soy sauce, sugar, sesame oil, salt, and pepper to create a marinade. Place the meat in a gallon-size resealable plastic bag. Pour the marinade over the meat, seal the bag, and place it in a large bowl. Marinate for at least 30 minutes at room temperature, or for up to 24 hours in the refrigerator for a more pronounced flavor. 2. Remove the meat from the marinade and place it in the air fryer baskets, distributing it between zone 1 and zone 2. Select zone 1 and choose the 'Roast' function. Set the temperature to 230ºC and the timer to 4 minutes. Press 'Match Cook' to synchronize zone 2 with zone 1's settings. Press 'Start/Pause' to begin the cooking process. shaking the baskets halfway through to ensure even cooking. Transfer the cooked meat to a plate; it should be medium-rare and still pink in the middle. Lightly cover with aluminum foil to keep warm. 3. In a large bowl, whisk together vinegar, vegetable oil, minced garlic, sugar, salt, and pepper to make the dressing. Add thinly sliced onion to the bowl and stir to combine. Add lettuce, tomatoes, and mint to the bowl, and toss until the salad is evenly coated with the dressing. Arrange the dressed salad on a serving platter. 4. Once the meat is cooked and the salad is prepared, arrange the cooked meat over the salad on the platter. Drizzle any accumulated juices from the plate over the meat to enhance the flavor. Serve the salad topped with lime wedges, a sprinkle of coarse salt, and cracked black pepper for an added touch of freshness and seasoning.

Barbecue Ribs

Prep time: 5 minutes | Cook time: 30 minutes | Serves 4

- 1 (900 g) rack pork loin Back Ribs
- 1 teaspoon onion granules
- 1 teaspoon garlic powder
- 1 teaspoon light brown sugar
- 1 teaspoon dried oregano
- Salt and freshly ground black pepper, to taste
- Cooking oil spray
- 120 ml barbecue sauce

1. Use a sharp knife to remove the thin membrane from the back of the ribs. Cut the rack in half, or as needed, so the ribs fit in the air fryer basket. The best way to do this is to cut the ribs into 4- or 5-rib sections. 2. In a small bowl, stir together the onion granules, garlic powder, brown sugar, and oregano and season with salt and pepper. Rub the spice seasoning onto the front and back of the ribs. 3. Cover the ribs with cling film or foil and let sit at room temperature for 30 minutes. 4. Insert the crisper plate into the zone 1 and zone2 baskets and the insert into the unit. Preheat the unit by selecting zone 1, select ROAST, setting the temperature to 180ºC, and setting the time to 3 minutes. Press MATCH COOK to match zone 2 setting to zone 1. Then, Select START/ PAUSE to begin. 5. Once the unit is preheated, spray the crisper plate with cooking oil. Place the ribs into the basket. It is okay to stack them. 6. Selecting zone 1, select ROAST, setting the temperature to 180ºC, and setting the time to 30 minutes. Press MATCH COOK to match zone 2 setting to zone 1. Then, Select START/PAUSE to begin. 7. After 15 minutes, press START/PAUSE to pause the air fryer. Flip the ribs. Resume cooking for 15 minutes, or until a food thermometer registers 88ºC. 8. When the cooking is complete, transfer the ribs to a serving dish. Drizzle the ribs with the barbecue sauce and serve.

Bacon Wrapped Pork with Apple Gravy

Prep time: 10 minutes | Cook time: 25 minutes | Serves 4

Pork:
- 1 tablespoons Dijon mustard
- 1 pork tenderloin
- 3 strips bacon

Apple Gravy:
- 3 tablespoons ghee, divided
- 1 small shallot, chopped
- 2 apples
- 1 tablespoon almond flour
- 235 ml vegetable stock
- ½ teaspoon Dijon mustard

1. Set the air fryer to preheat at 180ºC. 2. Generously spread Dijon mustard all over the pork tenderloin. Wrap the tenderloin with strips of bacon, ensuring the mustard layer is covered. 3. Place the mustard and bacon-wrapped tenderloin in the air fryer basket of zone 1. Cook for 12 minutes, using a meat thermometer to check for doneness (the internal temperature should reach 74ºC for medium doneness). 4. Select zone 1, choose the 'Roast' function, set the temperature to 180ºC, and set the timer for 12 minutes. Press 'Start/Pause' to begin the cooking process. 5. While the pork is cooking, prepare the sauce by heating 1 tablespoon of ghee in a pan. Add finely chopped shallots and cook for about 1 minute until they start to soften. 6. Add diced apples to the pan with shallots and continue cooking for 4 minutes until the apples begin to soften. 7. Stir in flour to make a roux, then gradually add stock while stirring well to combine. Add mustard to the sauce and continue stirring. 8. Allow the sauce to come to a bubble, then add the sautéed apples back into the sauce. Cook until the sauce thickens to your desired consistency. 9. Once the pork tenderloin is cooked, remove it from the air fryer and let it rest for 8 minutes before slicing. This allows the juices to redistribute within the meat, ensuring a moist and tender result. 10. Slice the rested pork tenderloin and serve it topped with the warm apple gravy.

Cantonese BBQ Pork

Prep time: 30 minutes | Cook time: 15 minutes | Serves 4

- 60 ml honey
- 2 tablespoons dark soy sauce
- 1 tablespoon sugar
- 1 tablespoon Shaoxing wine (rice cooking wine)
- 1 tablespoon hoisin sauce
- 2 teaspoons minced garlic
- 2 teaspoons minced fresh ginger
- 1 teaspoon Chinese five-spice powder
- 450 g fatty pork shoulder, cut into long, 1-inch-thick pieces

1. Prepare the Marinade: In a small microwave-safe bowl, mix together honey, soy sauce, sugar, wine, hoisin sauce, minced garlic, minced ginger, and five-spice powder. Microwave the mixture in 10-second intervals, stirring between each, until the honey is completely dissolved and the ingredients are well combined. 2. Marinate the Pork: Using a fork, pierce the pork slices in several places to allow the marinade to penetrate more effectively. Transfer the pork to a large bowl or a resealable plastic bag. Pour in half of the prepared marinade, reserving the other half for later use as a sauce. Toss the pork to ensure it is evenly coated. Marinate at room temperature for 30 minutes for a quick flavor infusion, or for up to 24 hours in the refrigerator for a deeper marinade effect. 3. Cook the Pork: Arrange the marinated pork slices in a single layer in the air fryer baskets of zone 1 and zone 2, ensuring they are not overlapping for even cooking. 4. Set the Air Fryer: Select zone 1 and choose the 'Roast' function. Set the temperature to 200ºC and the timer to 15 minutes. Press 'MATCH COOK' button to match zone 2 setting to zone 1. Then press 'Start/Pause' to begin cooking. The pork should be turned and basted with the remaining marinade halfway through the cooking time to enhance flavor and maintain moisture. 5. Prepare the Sauce: While the pork is cooking, to make the sauce thicker, microwave the reserved marinade on high for 45 to 60 seconds, stirring every 15 seconds, until it reaches a saucy consistency. 6. Rest and Serve: Once the pork is cooked, transfer it to a cutting board and let it rest for 10 minutes to allow the juices to settle. This will make the pork more tender and flavorful. After resting, brush the pork with the thickened sauce to serve.

Mongolian-Style Beef

Prep time: 10 minutes | Cook time: 10 minutes | Serves 4

- Oil, for spraying
- 30 g cornflour
- 450 g bavette or skirt steak, thinly sliced
- 140 g packed light brown sugar
- 120 ml soy sauce
- 2 teaspoons toasted sesame oil
- 1 tablespoon minced garlic
- ½ teaspoon ground ginger
- 120 ml water
- Cooked white rice or ramen noodles, for serving

1. Line the zone 1 and zone 2 air fryer baskets with parchment and spray lightly with oil. 2. Place the cornflour in a bowl and dredge the steak until evenly coated. Shake off any excess cornflour. 3. Place the steak in the prepared basketS and spray lightly with oil. 4. Select zone 1, select ROAST, set temperature to 200ºC, set time to 5 minutes. Press MATCH BUTTON to match zone 2 setting to zone 1. Then, press START/PAUSE to begin. After 5 minutes, flip, and cook for another 5 minutes. 5. In a small saucepan, combine the brown sugar, soy sauce, sesame oil, garlic, ginger, and water and bring to a boil over medium-high heat, stirring frequently. Remove from the heat. 6. Transfer the meat to the sauce and toss until evenly coated. Let sit for about 5 minutes so the steak absorbs the flavours. Serve with white rice or ramen noodles.

Beef Bavette Steak with Sage

Prep time: 13 minutes | Cook time: 7 minutes | Serves 2

- 80 ml sour cream
- 120 g spring onion, chopped
- 1 tablespoon mayonnaise
- 3 cloves garlic, smashed
- 450 g beef bavette or skirt steak, trimmed and cubed
- 2 tablespoons fresh sage, minced
- ½ teaspoon salt
- ⅓ teaspoon black pepper, or to taste

1. Season your meat with salt and pepper; arrange beef into zone 1 air fryer basket. 2. Stir in spring onions and garlic. Select zone 1, select ROAST, set temperature to 200ºC, set time to 7 minutes. Then, press START/PAUSE to begin. 3. Once your beef starts to tender, add the cream, mayonnaise, and sage; air fry an additional 8 minutes. Bon appétit!

Pork and Tricolor Vegetables Kebabs

Prep time: 1 hour 20 minutes | Cook time: 8 minutes per batch | Serves 4

For the Pork:
- 450 g pork steak, cut in cubes
- 1 tablespoon white wine vinegar
- 3 tablespoons steak sauce or brown sauce

For the Vegetable:
- 1 courgette, cut in cubes
- 1 butternut marrow, deseeded and cut in cubes
- 1 red pepper, cut in cubes
- 1 green pepper, cut in cubes
- Salt and ground black
- 60 ml soy sauce
- 1 teaspoon powdered chili
- 1 teaspoon red chilli flakes
- 2 teaspoons smoked paprika
- 1 teaspoon garlic salt

pepper, to taste
- Cooking spray
- Special Equipment:
- 4 bamboo skewers, soaked in water for at least 30 minutes

1. Marinate the Pork: Combine all the marinade ingredients in a large bowl. Add the pork pieces, ensuring they are fully submerged in the marinade. Cover the bowl with plastic wrap and refrigerate for at least 1 hour. 2. Preheat the Air Fryer: Preheat your Ninja Dual zone Air Fryer to 190ºC (374ºF) and lightly spritz the basket with cooking spray. 3. Prepare the Skewers: Remove the pork from the marinade. Alternate threading the pork pieces and vegetable chunks onto skewers. Season with salt and black pepper to taste. 4. Air Fry the Skewers: Arrange the skewers in the preheated zone 1 and zone 2 air fryer baskets without overcrowding. Lightly spritz with cooking spray. Select zone 1, choose the "AIR FRY" function, set the temperature to 190ºC (374ºF), and set the time to 8 minutes. Press MATCH COOK to match zone 2 setting to zone1. Then, Press START/PAUSE to begin cooking. Flip the skewers halfway through the cooking time to ensure even browning. You may need to cook in batches to avoid overcrowding the basket. 5. Serve: Once the pork is browned and the vegetables are lightly charred and tender, remove the skewers from the air fryer. Serve immediately.

Garlic Balsamic London Broil

Prep time: 30 minutes | Cook time: 8 to 10 minutes | Serves 8

- 900 g bavette or skirt steak
- 3 large garlic cloves, minced
- 3 tablespoons balsamic vinegar
- 3 tablespoons wholegrain mustard
- 2 tablespoons olive oil
- Sea salt and ground black pepper, to taste
- ½ teaspoon dried hot red pepper flakes

1. Lightly score both sides of the cleaned steaks with a knife to help the marinade penetrate the meat. 2. In a bowl, thoroughly combine the olive oil, soy sauce, Worcestershire sauce, minced garlic, dried rosemary, dried thyme, black pepper, and salt. Massage this mixture into the meat to coat it on all sides. Cover and let it marinate in the refrigerator for at least 3 hours. 3. Preheat your Ninja Dual zone Air Fryer to 200ºC (392ºF). 4. Place the marinated steaks in the zone 1 air fryer basket. Select zone 1, choose the "ROAST" function, set the temperature to 200ºC (392ºF), and the time to 15 minutes. Press START/PAUSE to begin cooking. 5. After 15 minutes, flip the steaks over and continue cooking for another 10-12 minutes, or until the steaks reach your desired level of doneness. 6. Remove the steaks from the air fryer and let them rest for 5 minutes before serving to allow the juices to redistribute.

Chapter 4 Beef, Pork, and Lamb

Chapter 5　Fish and Seafood

Chapter 5 Fish and Seafood

New Orleans-Style Crab Cakes

Prep time: 10 minutes | Cook time: 8 to 10 minutes | Serves 4

- 95 g bread crumbs
- 2 teaspoons Creole Seasoning
- 1 teaspoon dry mustard
- 1 teaspoon salt
- 1 teaspoon freshly ground black pepper
- 360 g crab meat
- 2 large eggs, beaten
- 1 teaspoon butter, melted
- ⅓ cup minced onion
- Cooking spray
- Tartar Sauce, for serving

1. Preheat the air fryer to 180ºC. Line the zone 1 and zone 2 air fryer baskets with baking papers. 2. In a medium bowl, whisk the bread crumbs, Creole Seasoning, dry mustard, salt, and pepper until blended. Add the crab meat, eggs, butter, and onion. Stir until blended. Shape the crab mixture into 8 patties. 3. Place the crab cakes on the baking papers and spritz with oil. 4. Select zone 1, Select ROAST, set time to 4 minutes, set temperature to 180ºC. Press MATCH COOK to match zone 2 setting to zone 1. Then, Press START/PAUSE to begin. 5. Flip the cakes, spritz them with oil, and air fry for 4 to 6 minutes more until the outsides are firm and a fork inserted into the center comes out clean. Serve with the Tartar Sauce.

Cucumber and Salmon Salad

Prep time: 10 minutes | Cook time: 8 to 10 minutes | Serves 2

- 455 g salmon fillet
- 1½ tablespoons olive oil, divided
- 1 tablespoon sherry vinegar
- 1 tablespoon capers, rinsed and drained
- 1 seedless cucumber, thinly sliced
- ¼ white onion, thinly sliced
- 2 tablespoons chopped fresh parsley
- Salt and freshly ground black pepper, to taste

1. Preheat the air fryer to 200ºC. 2. Lightly coat the salmon with ½ tablespoon of the olive oil. 3. Place skin-side down in the zone 1 air fryer basket. Select zone 1, Select ROAST, Set temperature to 200ºC, set time to 8-10 minutes. Then, press START/PAUSE to begin until the fish is opaque and flakes easily with a fork. Transfer the salmon to a plate and let cool to room temperature. Remove the skin and carefully flake the fish into bite-size chunks. 4. In a small bowl, whisk the remaining 1 tablespoon olive oil and the vinegar until thoroughly combined. Add the flaked fish, capers, cucumber, onion, and parsley. Season to taste with salt and freshly ground black pepper. Toss gently to coat. Serve immediately or cover and refrigerate for up to 4 hours.

Chilli Prawns

Prep time: 10 minutes | Cook time: 8 minutes | Serves 2

- 8 prawns, peeled and deveined
- Salt and black pepper, to taste
- ½ teaspoon ground cayenne pepper
- ½ teaspoon garlic powder
- ½ teaspoon ground cumin
- ½ teaspoon red chilli flakes
- Cooking spray

1. Preheat the air fryer to 170ºC. Spritz the zone 1 air fryer basket with cooking spray. 2. Toss the remaining ingredients in a large bowl until the prawns are well coated. 3. Spread the coated prawns evenly in the zone 1 basket and spray them with cooking spray. 4. Select zone 1, Select ROAST, set temperature to 170ºC, set time to 8 minutes. Then, press START/PAUSE to begin. Flipping the prawns halfway through, or until the prawns are pink. 5. Remove the prawns from the basket to a plate.

Spicy Air Fried Old Bay Shrimp

Prep time: 7 minutes | Cook time: 10 minutes | Makes 475 ml

- ½ teaspoon Old Bay or all-purpose seasoning
- 1 teaspoon ground cayenne pepper
- ½ teaspoon paprika
- 1 tablespoon olive oil
- ⅛ teaspoon salt
- 230 g shrimps, peeled and deveined
- Juice of half a lemon

1. Preheat the air fryer to 200ºC. 2.Combine the seasoning, cayenne pepper, paprika, olive oil, and salt in a large bowl, then add the shrimps and toss to coat well. 3.Put the shrimps in the preheated zone 1 and zone 2 air fryer baskets. 4. Select zone 1, Select ROAST, Set temperature to 200ºC, set time to 10 minutes. Press MATCH COOK to match zone 2 setting to zone 1. Then, press START/PAUSE to begin until opaque. 5. Flip the shrimps halfway through. 6.Serve the shrimps with lemon juice on top.

Thai Prawn Skewers with Peanut Dipping Sauce

Prep time: 15 minutes | Cook time: 6 minutes | Serves 2

- Salt and pepper, to taste
- 340 g extra-large prawns, peeled and deveined
- 1 tablespoon vegetable oil
- 1 teaspoon honey
- ½ teaspoon grated lime zest plus 1 tablespoon juice, plus lime wedges for serving
- 6 (6-inch) wooden skewers
- 3 tablespoons creamy peanut butter
- 3 tablespoons hot tap water
- 1 tablespoon chopped fresh coriander
- 1 teaspoon fish sauce

1. Preheat the air fryer to 200°C. 2. Dissolve 2 tablespoons salt in 1 litre cold water in a large container. Add prawns, cover, and refrigerate for 15 minutes. 3. Remove prawns from brine and pat dry with paper towels. Whisk oil, honey, lime zest, and ¼ teaspoon pepper together in a large bowl. Add prawns and toss to coat. Thread prawns onto skewers, leaving about ¼ inch between each prawns (3 or 4 prawns per skewer). 4. Arrange skewers in zone 1 and zone 2 air fryer baskets. Parallel to each other and spaced evenly apart. Select zone 1, Select ROAST, Set temperature to 200°C, set time to 6-8 minutes. Press MATCH COOK to match zone 2 setting to zone 1. Then, press START/PAUSE to begin. Air fry until prawns are opaque throughout, flipping and rotating skewers halfway through cooking. 5. Whisk peanut butter, hot tap water, lime juice, coriander, and fish sauce together in a bowl until smooth. Serve skewers with peanut dipping sauce and lime wedges.

chilli Lime Prawns

Prep time: 5 minutes | Cook time: 5 minutes | Serves 4

- 455 g medium prawns, peeled and deveined
- 1 tablespoon salted butter, melted
- 2 teaspoons chilli powder
- ¼ teaspoon garlic powder
- ¼ teaspoon salt
- ¼ teaspoon ground black pepper
- ½ small lime, zested and juiced, divided

1. In a medium bowl, toss prawns with butter, then sprinkle with chilli powder, garlic powder, salt, pepper, and lime zest. 2. Place prawns into ungreased zone 1 and zone 2 air fryer basket. Select zone 1, Select ROAST, Set temperature to 200°C, set time to 5 minutes. Press MATCH COOK to match zone 2 setting to zone 1. Then, press START/PAUSE to begin. 3. Prawns will be firm and form a "C" shape when done. Transfer prawns to a large serving dish and drizzle with lime juice. Serve warm.

Savoury Prawns

Prep time: 5 minutes | Cook time: 8 to 10 minutes | Serves 4

- 455 g fresh large prawns, peeled and deveined
- 1 tablespoon avocado oil
- 2 teaspoons minced garlic, divided
- ½ teaspoon red pepper flakes
- Sea salt and freshly ground black pepper, to taste
- 2 tablespoons unsalted butter, melted
- 2 tablespoons chopped fresh parsley

1. Place the prawns in a large bowl and toss with the avocado oil, 1 teaspoon of minced garlic, and red pepper flakes. Season with salt and pepper. 2. Arrange the prawns in a single layer in the zone 1 and zone 2 air fryer baskets. 3. Select zone 1, Select ROAST, set temperature to 180°C, set time to 6 minutes. Press MATCH COOK to match zone 2 setting to zone 1. Then, press START/PAUSE to begin. 4. Flip the prawns and cook for 2 to 4 minutes more, until the internal temperature of the prawns reaches 50°C. (The time it takes to cook will depend on the size of the prawns.) 5. While the prawns are cooking, melt the butter in a small saucepan over medium heat and stir in the remaining 1 teaspoon of garlic. 6. Transfer the cooked prawns to a large bowl, add the garlic butter, and toss well. Top with the parsley and serve warm.

Herbed Prawns Pita

Prep time: 5 minutes | Cook time: 8 minutes | Serves 4

- 455 g medium prawns, peeled and deveined
- 2 tablespoons olive oil
- 1 teaspoon dried oregano
- ½ teaspoon dried thyme
- ½ teaspoon garlic powder
- ¼ teaspoon onion powder
- ½ teaspoon salt
- ¼ teaspoon black pepper
- 4 whole wheat pitas
- 110 g feta cheese, crumbled
- 75 g shredded lettuce
- 1 tomato, diced
- 45 g black olives, sliced
- 1 lemon

1. Preheat the oven to 190°C. 2. In a medium bowl, combine the prawns with the olive oil, oregano, thyme, garlic powder, onion powder, salt, and black pepper. 3. Pour prawns in a single layer in the zone 1 and zone 2 air fryer baskets. 4. Select zone 1, Select ROAST, Set temperature to 190°C, set time to 6-8 minutes. Press MATCH COOK to match zone 2 setting to zone 1. Then, press START/PAUSE to begin. 5. Remove from the air fryer and divide into warmed pitas with feta, lettuce, tomato, olives, and a squeeze of lemon.

Blackened Red Snapper

Prep time: 13 minutes | Cook time: 8 to 10 minutes | Serves 4

- 1½ teaspoons black pepper
- ¼ teaspoon thyme
- ¼ teaspoon garlic powder
- ⅛ teaspoon cayenne pepper
- 1 teaspoon olive oil
- 4 red snapper fillet portions, skin on, 110 g each
- 4 thin slices lemon
- Cooking spray

1. Mix the spices and oil together to make a paste. Rub into both sides of the fish. 2. Spray the air fryer basket with nonstick cooking spray and lay snapper steaks in basket, skin-side down. 3. Place a lemon slice on each piece of fish. Arrange fish into zone 1 and zone 2 baskets. 4. Select zone 1, Select ROAST, Set temperature to 200ºC, set time to 8-10 minutes. Press MATCH COOK to match zone 2 setting to zone 1. Then, press START/PAUSE to begin. The fish will not flake when done, but it should be white through the center.

Fish Sandwich with Tartar Sauce

Prep time: 10 minutes | Cook time: 17 minutes | Serves 2

Tartar Sauce:
- 115 g mayonnaise
- 2 tablespoons onion granules
- 1 dill gherkin spear, finely chopped

Fish:
- 2 tablespoons plain flour
- 1 egg, lightly beaten
- 120 g panko
- 2 teaspoons lemon pepper
- 2 teaspoons gherkin juice
- ¼ teaspoon salt
- ⅛ teaspoon ground black pepper
- 2 tilapia fillets
- Cooking spray
- 2 soft sub rolls

1. Preheat the air fryer to 200ºC. 2. In a small bowl, combine the mayonnaise, onion granules, pickle, gherkin juice, salt, and pepper. 3. Whisk to combine and chill in the refrigerator while you make the fish. 4. Place a baking paper liner in the air fryer basket. 5. Scoop the flour out onto a plate; set aside. 6. Put the beaten egg in a medium shallow bowl. 7. On another plate, mix to combine the panko and lemon pepper. 8. Dredge the tilapia fillets in the flour, then dip in the egg, and then press into the panko mixture. 9. Place the prepared fillets on the liner in the zone 1 and zone 2 air fryer baskets in a single layer. 10. Spray lightly with cooking spray. Select zone 1, Select ROAST, Set temperature to 200ºC, set time to 8 minutes. Press MATCH COOK to match zone 2 setting to zone 1. Then, press START/PAUSE to begin. Carefully flip the fillets, spray with more cooking spray, and air fry for an additional 9 minutes, until golden and crispy. 11. Place each cooked fillet in a sub roll, top with a little bit of tartar sauce, and serve.

Honey-Balsamic Salmon

Prep time: 5 minutes | Cook time: 8 minutes | Serves 2

- Olive or vegetable oil, for spraying
- 2 (170 g) salmon fillets
- 60 ml balsamic vinegar
- 2 tablespoons honey
- 2 teaspoons red pepper flakes
- 2 teaspoons olive oil
- ½ teaspoon salt
- ¼ teaspoon freshly ground black pepper

1. Line the air fryer basket with baking paper and spray lightly with oil. 2. Place the salmon in the prepared zone 1 basket. 3. In a small bowl, whisk together the balsamic vinegar, honey, red pepper flakes, olive oil, salt, and black pepper. Brush the mixture over the salmon. 4. Select zone 1, Select ROAST, set temperature to 200ºC, set time to 7-8 minutes. Then, press START/PAUSE to begin until the internal temperature reaches 64ºC. Serve immediately.

Steamed Tuna with Lemongrass

Prep time: 10 minutes | Cook time: 10 minutes | Serves 4

- 4 small tuna steaks
- 2 tablespoons low-sodium soy sauce
- 2 teaspoons sesame oil
- 2 teaspoons rice wine vinegar
- 1 teaspoon grated peeled fresh ginger
- ⅛ teaspoon freshly ground black pepper
- 1 stalk lemongrass, bent in half
- 3 tablespoons freshly squeezed lemon juice

1. Place the tuna steaks on a plate. 2. In a small bowl, whisk the soy sauce, sesame oil, vinegar, and ginger until combined. Pour this mixture over the tuna and gently rub it into both sides. Sprinkle the fish with the pepper. Let marinate for 10 minutes. 3. Insert the crisper plate into the zone 1 and zone 2 baskets, and the basket into the unit. Preheat the unit to 200ºC. 4. Once the unit is preheated, place the lemongrass into the basket and top it with the tuna steaks. Drizzle the tuna with the lemon juice and 1 tablespoon of water. 5. Select zone 1, Select ROAST, set temperature to 200ºC, set time to 10 minutes. Press MATCH COOK to match zone 2 setting to zone 1. Then, press START/PAUSE to begin. 6. When the cooking is complete, a food thermometer inserted into the tuna should register at least 64ºC. Discard the lemongrass and serve the tuna.

Chapter 5 Fish and Seafood

Balsamic Tilapia

Prep time: 5 minutes | Cook time: 15 minutes | Serves 4

- 4 tilapia fillets, boneless
- 2 tablespoons balsamic vinegar
- 1 teaspoon avocado oil
- 1 teaspoon dried basil

1. Sprinkle the tilapia fillets with balsamic vinegar, avocado oil, and dried basil. 2. Then put the fillets in the zone 1 and zone 2 air fryer baskets. 3. Select zone 1, Select ROAST, Set temperature to 190ºC, set time to 15 minutes. Press MATCH COOK to match zone 2 setting to zone 1. Then, press START/PAUSE to begin.

Almond Catfish

Prep time: 10 minutes | Cook time: 12 minutes | Serves 4

- 900 g catfish fillet
- 25 g almond flour
- 2 eggs, beaten
- 1 teaspoon salt
- 1 teaspoon avocado oil

1. Sprinkle the catfish fillet with salt and dip in the eggs. 2. Then coat the fish in the almond flour and put in the zone 1 and zone 2 air fryer baskets. Sprinkle the fish with avocado oil. 3. Select zone 1, Select ROAST, Set temperature to 190ºC, set time to 6 minutes. Press MATCH COOK to match zone 2 setting to zone 1. Then, press START/PAUSE to begin. 4. After 6 minutes, open the zone 1 and zone 2 ai fryers, flip the fish over. Select zone 1, Select ROAST, Set temperature to 190ºC, set time to 6 minutes. Press MATCH COOK to match zone 2 setting to zone 1. Then, press START/PAUSE to cook the other side.

Cajun Catfish Cakes with Cheese

Prep time: 5 minutes | Cook time: 35 minutes | Serves 4

- 2 catfish fillets
- 85 g butter
- 150 g shredded Parmesan cheese
- 150 g shredded Swiss cheese
- 120 ml buttermilk
- 1 teaspoon baking powder
- 1 teaspoon baking soda
- 1 teaspoon Cajun seasoning

1. Bring a pot of salted water to a boil. Add the catfish fillets to the boiling water and let them boil for 5 minutes until they become opaque. 2. Remove the fillets from the pot to a mixing bowl and flake them into small pieces with a fork. 3. Add the remaining ingredients to the bowl of fish and stir until well incorporated. 4. Divide the fish mixture into 12 equal portions and shape each portion into a patty. 5. Preheat the air fryer to 190ºC. 6. Arrange the patties in the zone 1 and zone 2 air fryer baskets. Select zone 1, Select ROAST, Set temperature to 190ºC, set time to 15 minutes. Press MATCH COOK to match zone 2 setting to zone 1. Then, press START/PAUSE to begin until golden brown and cooked through. Flip the patties halfway through the cooking time. 7. Let the patties sit for 5 minutes and serve.

Sesame-Crusted Tuna Steak

Prep time: 5 minutes | Cook time: 8 minutes | Serves 2

- 2 tuna steaks, 170 g each
- 1 tablespoon coconut oil, melted
- ½ teaspoon garlic powder
- 2 teaspoons white sesame seeds
- 2 teaspoons black sesame seeds

1. Brush each tuna steak with coconut oil and sprinkle with garlic powder. 2. In a large bowl, mix sesame seeds and then press each tuna steak into them, covering the steak as completely as possible. Place tuna steaks into the zone 1 and zone 2 air fryer baskets. 3. Select zone 1, Select ROAST, Set temperature to 200ºC, set time to 8 minutes. Press MATCH COOK to match zone 2 setting to zone 1. Then, press START/PAUSE to begin. 4. Flip the steaks halfway through the cooking time. Steaks will be well-done at 64ºC internal temperature. Serve warm.

Fish Gratin

Prep time: 30 minutes | Cook time: 17 minutes | Serves 4

- 1 tablespoon avocado oil
- 455 g hake fillets
- 1 teaspoon garlic powder
- Sea salt and ground white pepper, to taste
- 2 tablespoons shallots, chopped
- 1 pepper, seeded and chopped
- 110 g cottage cheese
- 120 ml sour cream
- 1 egg, well whisked
- 1 teaspoon yellow mustard
- 1 tablespoon lime juice
- 60 g Swiss cheese, shredded

1. Brush the bottom and sides of a casserole dish with avocado oil. Add the hake fillets to the casserole dish and sprinkle with garlic powder, salt, and pepper. 2. Add the chopped shallots and peppers. 3. In a mixing bowl, thoroughly combine the Cottage cheese, sour cream, egg, mustard, and lime juice. Pour the mixture over fish and spread evenly. 4. Select zone 1, Select ROAST, Set temperature to 190ºC, set time to 10 minutes. Then, press START/PAUSE to begin. 5. Top with the Swiss cheese and cook an additional 7 minutes. Let it rest for 10 minutes before slicing and serving. Bon appétit!

Catfish Bites

Prep time: 15 minutes | Cook time: 20 minutes | Serves 4

- Olive or vegetable oil, for spraying
- 455 g catfish fillets, cut into 2-inch pieces
- 235 ml buttermilk
- 35 g cornmeal
- 20 g plain flour
- 2 teaspoons Creole seasoning
- 120 ml yellow mustard

1. Line the zone 1 and zone 2 air fryer baskets with baking paper and spray lightly with oil. 2. Place the catfish pieces and buttermilk in a zip-top plastic bag, seal, and refrigerate for about 10 minutes. 3. In a shallow bowl, mix together the cornmeal, flour, and Creole seasoning. 4. Remove the catfish from the bag and pat dry with a paper towel. 5. Spread the mustard on all sides of the catfish, then dip them in the cornmeal mixture until evenly coated. 6. Place the catfish in the prepared zone 1 and zone 2 baskets. Spray lightly with oil. 7. Select zone 1, Select ROAST, Set temperature to 200°C, set time to 10 minutes. Press MATCH COOK to match zone 2 setting to zone 1. Then, press START/PAUSE to begin. Flip carefully, spray with oil, and cook for another 10 minutes. Serve immediately.

Coconut Prawns with Spicy Dipping Sauce

Prep time: 15 minutes | Cook time: 8 minutes | Serves 4

- 70 g pork scratchings
- 70 g desiccated, unsweetened coconut
- 45 g coconut flour
- 1 teaspoon onion powder
- 1 teaspoon garlic powder
- 2 eggs
- 680 g large prawns, peeled and deveined
- ½ teaspoon salt
- ¼ teaspoon freshly ground black pepper
- Spicy Dipping Sauce:
- 115 g mayonnaise
- 2 tablespoons Sriracha
- Zest and juice of ½ lime
- 1 clove garlic, minced

1. Preheat the air fryer to 200°C. 2. In a food processor fitted with a metal blade, combine the pork scratchings and desiccated coconut. Pulse until the mixture resembles coarse crumbs. Transfer to a shallow bowl. 3. In another shallow bowl, combine the coconut flour, onion powder, and garlic powder; mix until thoroughly combined. 4. In a third shallow bowl, whisk the eggs until slightly frothy. 5. In a large bowl, season the prawns with the salt and pepper, tossing gently to coat. 6. Working a few pieces at a time, dredge the prawns in the flour mixture, followed by the eggs, and finishing with the pork rind crumb mixture. Arrange the prawns on a baking sheet until ready to air fry. 7. Arrange the prawns in a single layer in the zone 1 and zone 2 air fryer baskets. Select zone 1, Select ROAST, Set temperature to 200°C, set time to 8 minutes. Press MATCH COOK to match zone 2 setting to zone 1. Then, press START/PAUSE to begin. Pausing halfway through the cooking time to turn the prawns. 8. To make the sauce: In a small bowl, combine the mayonnaise, Sriracha, lime zest and juice, and garlic. Whisk until thoroughly combined. Serve alongside the prawns.

Lemon-Pepper Trout

Prep time: 5 minutes | Cook time: 15 minutes | Serves 4

- 4 trout fillets
- 2 tablespoons olive oil
- ½ teaspoon salt
- 1 teaspoon black pepper
- 2 garlic cloves, sliced
- 1 lemon, sliced, plus additional wedges for serving

1. Preheat the air fryer to 190°C. 2. Brush each fillet with olive oil on both sides and season with salt and pepper. Place the fillets in an even layer in the zone 1 and zone 2 air fryer baskets. 3. Place the sliced garlic over the tops of the trout fillets, then top the garlic with lemon slices. Select zone 1, Select ROAST, Set temperature to 190°C, set time to 12-15 minutes. Press MATCH COOK to match zone 2 setting to zone 1. Then, press START/PAUSE to begin until it has reached an internal temperature of 64°C. 4. Serve with fresh lemon wedges.

Roasted Halibut Steaks with Parsley

Prep time: 5 minutes | Cook time: 10 minutes | Serves 4

- 455 g halibut steaks
- 60 ml vegetable oil
- 2½ tablespoons Worcester sauce
- 2 tablespoons honey
- 2 tablespoons vermouth or white wine vinegar
- 1 tablespoon freshly squeezed lemon juice
- 1 tablespoon fresh parsley leaves, coarsely chopped
- Salt and pepper, to taste
- 1 teaspoon dried basil

1. Preheat the air fryer to 200°C. 2. Put all the ingredients in a large mixing dish and gently stir until the fish is coated evenly. 3. Transfer the fish to the zone 1 and zone 2 air fryer baskets. Select zone 1, Select ROAST, Set temperature to 200°C, set time to 10 minutes. Press MATCH COOK to match zone 2 setting to zone 1. Then, press START/PAUSE to begin. 4. Flipping the fish halfway through, or until the fish reaches an internal temperature of at least 64°C on a meat thermometer. 5. Let the fish cool for 5 minutes and serve.

Sea Bass with Avocado Cream

Prep time: 30 minutes | Cook time: 9 minutes | Serves 4

Fish Fillets:
- 1½ tablespoons balsamic vinegar
- 120 ml vegetable broth
- ⅓ teaspoon shallot powder
- 1 tablespoon coconut aminos, or tamari
- 4 Sea Bass fillets
- 1 teaspoon ground black pepper
- 1½ tablespoons olive oil
- Fine sea salt, to taste
- ⅓ teaspoon garlic powder

Avocado Cream:
- 2 tablespoons Greek-style yoghurt
- 1 clove garlic, peeled and minced
- 1 teaspoon ground black pepper
- ½ tablespoon olive oil
- 80 ml vegetable broth
- 1 avocado
- ½ teaspoon lime juice
- ⅓ teaspoon fine sea salt

1. In a bowl, wash and pat the fillets dry using some paper towels. Add all the seasonings. In another bowl, stir in the remaining ingredients for the fish fillets. 2. Add the seasoned fish fillets; cover and let the fillets marinate in your refrigerator at least 3 hours. 3. Then, arrange the fillets in zone 1 and zone 2 baskets. 4. Select zone 1, Select ROAST, Set temperature to 160ºC, set time to 9 minutes. Press MATCH COOK to match zone 2 setting to zone 1. Then, press START/PAUSE to begin. 5. In the meantime, prepare the avocado sauce by mixing all the ingredients with an immersion blender or regular blender. Serve the sea bass fillets topped with the avocado sauce. Enjoy!

Fish Cakes

Prep time: 30 minutes | Cook time: 10 to 12 minutes | Serves 4

- 1 large russet potato, mashed
- 340 g cod or other white fish
- Salt and pepper, to taste
- Olive or vegetable oil for misting or cooking spray
- 1 large egg
- 50 g potato starch
- 30 g panko breadcrumbs
- 1 tablespoon fresh chopped chives
- 2 tablespoons minced onion

1. Peel potatoes, cut into cubes, and cook on stovetop till soft. 2. Salt and pepper raw fish to taste. Arrange the fish into zone 1 and zone 2 air fryer baskets. Mist with oil or cooking spray. 3. Select zone 1, Select ROAST, Set temperature to 180ºC, set time to 6-8 minutes. Press MATCH COOK to match zone 2 setting to zone 1. Then, press START/PAUSE to begin until fish flakes easily. 4. Transfer fish to a plate and break apart to cool. 5. Beat egg in a shallow dish. 6. Place potato starch in another shallow dish, and panko crumbs in a third dish. 7. When potatoes are done, drain in colander and rinse with cold water. 8. In a large bowl, mash the potatoes and stir in the chives and onion. Add salt and pepper to taste, then stir in the fish. 9. If needed, stir in a tablespoon of the beaten egg to help bind the mixture. 10. Shape into 8 small, fat patties. Dust lightly with potato starch, dip in egg, and roll in panko crumbs. Spray both sides with oil or cooking spray. 11. Select zone 1, Select ROAST, Set temperature to 200ºC, set time to 10-12 minutes. Press MATCH COOK to match zone 2 setting to zone 1. Then, press START/PAUSE to complete cooking.

Tuna Steak

Prep time: 10 minutes | Cook time: 12 minutes | Serves 4

- 455 g tuna steaks, boneless and cubed
- 1 tablespoon mustard
- 1 tablespoon avocado oil
- 1 tablespoon apple cider vinegar

1. Mix avocado oil with mustard and apple cider vinegar. 2. Then brush tuna steaks with mustard mixture and put in the zone 1 and zone 2 air fryer basket. 3. Select zone 1, Select ROAST, Set temperature to 180ºC, set time to 6 minutes. Press MATCH COOK to match zone 2 setting to zone 1. Then, press START/PAUSE to begin. 4. After 6 minutes, open the zone 1 and zone 2 ai fryers, flip the fish over. Select zone 1, Select ROAST, Set temperature to 180ºC, set time to 6 minutes. Press MATCH COOK to match zone 2 setting to zone 1. Then, press START/PAUSE to cook the other side

Crab Cakes

Prep time: 10 minutes | Cook time: 10 minutes | Serves 4

- 2 tins lump crab meat, 170 g each
- ¼ cup blanched finely ground almond flour
- 1 large egg
- 2 tablespoons full-fat mayonnaise
- ½ teaspoon Dijon mustard
- ½ tablespoon lemon juice
- ½ medium green pepper, seeded and chopped
- 235 g chopped spring onion
- ½ teaspoon Old Bay seasoning

1. In a large bowl, combine all ingredients. Form into four balls and flatten into patties. Place patties into the zone 1 and zone 2 air fryer baskest. 2. Select zone 1, Select ROAST, Set temperature to 180ºC, set time to 10 minutes. Press MATCH COOK to match zone 2 setting to zone 1. Then, press START/PAUSE to begin. 3. Flip patties halfway through the cooking time. Serve warm.

Teriyaki Shrimp Skewers

Prep time: 10 minutes | Cook time: 6 minutes | Makes 12 skewered shrimp

- 1½ tablespoons mirin
- 1½ teaspoons ginger paste
- 1½ tablespoons soy sauce
- 12 large shrimp, peeled and deveined
- 1 large egg
- 90 g panko breadcrumbs
- Cooking spray

1. Combine the mirin, ginger paste, and soy sauce in a large bowl. 2. Stir to mix well. 3. Dunk the shrimp in the bowl of mirin mixture, then wrap the bowl in plastic and refrigerate for 1 hour to marinate. 4. Preheat the air fryer to 200°C. 5. Spritz the zone 1 and zone 2 air fryer baskets with cooking spray. 6. Run twelve 4-inch skewers through each shrimp. 7. Whisk the egg in the bowl of marinade to combine well. 8. Pour the breadcrumbs on a plate. 9. Dredge the shrimp skewers in the egg mixture, then shake the excess off and roll over the breadcrumbs to coat well. 10. Arrange the shrimp skewers in the preheated zone 1 and zone 2 air fryer and spritz with cooking spray. 11. Select zone 1, Select ROAST, Set temperature to 200°C, set time to 6 minutes. Press MATCH COOK to match zone 2 setting to zone 1. Then, press START/PAUSE to begin until the shrimp are opaque and firm. 12. Flip the shrimp skewers halfway through. 13. Serve immediately.

Pesto Fish Pie

Prep time: 15 minutes | Cook time: 15 minutes | Serves 4

- 2 tablespoons prepared pesto
- 60 ml single cream
- 20 g grated Parmesan cheese
- 1 teaspoon kosher or coarse sea salt
- 1 teaspoon black pepper
- Vegetable oil spray
- 280 g frozen chopped spinach, thawed and squeezed dry
- 455 g firm white fish, cut into 2-inch chunks
- 115 g cherry tomatoes, quartered
- Plain flour
- ½ sheet frozen puff pastry (from a 490 g package), thawed

1. In a small bowl, combine the pesto, single cream, Parmesan, salt, and pepper. Stir until well combined; set aside. 2. Spray the zone 1 baking pan with vegetable oil spray. Arrange the spinach evenly across the bottom of the pan. Top with the fish and tomatoes. Pour the pesto mixture evenly over everything. 3. On a lightly floured surface, roll the puff pastry sheet into a circle. Place the pastry on top of the pan and tuck it in around the edges of the pan. (Or, do what I do and stretch it with your hands and then pat it into place.) 4. Place the pan in the air fryer basket. Select zone 1, Select ROAST, Set temperature to 200°C, set time to 15 minutes. Then, press START/PAUSE to begin until the pastry is well browned. Let stand 5 minutes before serving.

Salmon Fritters with Courgette

Prep time: 15 minutes | Cook time: 12 minutes | Serves 4

- 2 tablespoons almond flour
- 1 courgette, grated
- 1 egg, beaten
- 170 g salmon fillet, diced
- 1 teaspoon avocado oil
- ½ teaspoon ground black pepper

1. Mix almond flour with courgette, egg, salmon, and ground black pepper. 2. Then make the fritters from the salmon mixture. 3. Sprinkle the zone 1 and zone 2 air fryer basket with avocado oil and put the fritters inside. 4. Select zone 1, Select ROAST, set temperature to 190 °C, set time to 6 minutes. Press MATCH COOK to match zone 2 setting to zone 1. Then, press START/PAUSE to begin. 5. After 6 minutes, flip them over, Select zone 1, Select ROAST, set temperature to 190 °C, set time to 6 minutes. Press MATCH COOK to match zone 2 setting to zone 1. Then, press START/PAUSE to cook the other side.

Fried Catfish with Dijon Sauce

Prep time: 20 minutes | Cook time: 7 minutes | Serves 4

- 4 tablespoons butter, melted
- 2 teaspoons Worcestershire sauce, divided
- 1 teaspoon lemon pepper
- 60 g panko bread crumbs
- 4 catfish fillets, 110g each
- Cooking spray
- 120 ml sour cream
- 1 tablespoon Dijon mustard

1. In a shallow bowl, stir together the melted butter, 1 teaspoon of Worcestershire sauce, and the lemon pepper. Place the bread crumbs in another shallow bowl. 2. One at a time, dip both sides of the fillets in the butter mixture, then the bread crumbs, coating thoroughly. 3. Preheat the air fryer to 150°C. Line the zone 1 and zone 2 air fryer baskets with baking papers. 4. Place the coated fish on the baking papers and spritz with oil. 5. Select zone 1, Select ROAST, set temperature to 150°C, set time to 4 minutes. Press MATCH COOK to match zone 2 setting to zone 1. Then, press START/PAUSE to begin. 6. Flip the fish, spritz it with oil, and bake for 3 to 6 minutes more, depending on the thickness of the fillets, until the fish flakes easily with a fork. 7. In a small bowl, stir together the sour cream, Dijon, and remaining 1 teaspoon of Worcestershire sauce. This sauce tin be made 1 day in advance and refrigerated before serving. Serve with the fried fish.

Chapter 5 Fish and Seafood

South Indian Fried Fish

Prep time: 20 minutes | Cook time: 8 minutes | Serves 4

- 2 tablespoons olive oil
- 2 tablespoons fresh lime or lemon juice
- 1 teaspoon minced fresh ginger
- 1 clove garlic, minced
- 1 teaspoon ground turmeric
- ½ teaspoon kosher or coarse sea salt
- ¼ to ½ teaspoon cayenne pepper
- 455 g tilapia fillets (2 to 3 fillets)
- Olive oil spray
- Lime or lemon wedges (optional)

1. In a large bowl, combine the oil, lime juice, ginger, garlic, turmeric, salt, and cayenne. Stir until well combined; set aside. 2. Cut each tilapia fillet into three or four equal-size pieces. Add the fish to the bowl and gently mix until all of the fish is coated in the marinade. Marinate for 10 to 15 minutes at room temperature. (Don't marinate any longer or the acid in the lime juice will "cook" the fish.) 3. Spray the zone 1 and zone 2 air fryer basketS with olive oil spray. Place the fish in the two baskets and spray the fish. 4. Select zone 1, Select ROAST, Set temperature to 160°C, set time to 3 minutes. Press MATCH COOK to match zone 2 setting to zone 1. Then, press START/PAUSE to partially cook the fish. 5. Select zone 1, Select ROAST, increase temperature to 200°C, set time to 5 minutes. Press MATCH COOK to match zone 2 setting to zone 1. Then, press START/PAUSE to finish cooking and crisp up the fish. (Thinner pieces of fish will cook faster so you may want to check at the 3-minute mark of the second cooking time and remove those that are cooked through, and then add them back toward the end of the second cooking time to crisp.) 6. Carefully remove the fish from the baskets. Serve hot, with lemon wedges if desired.

Chapter 6

Poultry

Chapter 6 Poultry

Easy Turkey Tenderloin

Prep time: 20 minutes | Cook time: 30 minutes | Serves 4

- Olive oil
- ½ teaspoon paprika
- ½ teaspoon garlic powder
- ½ teaspoon salt
- ½ teaspoon freshly ground black pepper
- Pinch cayenne pepper
- 680 g turkey breast tenderloin

1. Spray the air fryer basket lightly with olive oil. 2. In a small bowl, combine the paprika, garlic powder, salt, black pepper, and cayenne pepper. Rub the mixture all over the turkey. 3. Place the turkey in the air fryer basket and lightly spray with olive oil. 4. Select zone 1, Select ROAST, Set temperature to 190ºC, set time to 15 minutes. Then, press START/PAUSE to begin. 5. Flip the turkey over and lightly spray with olive oil. Air fry until the internal temperature reaches at least 80ºC for an additional 10 to 15 minutes. 6. Let the turkey rest for 10 minutes before slicing and serving.

Sweet Chili Spiced Chicken

Prep time: 10 minutes | Cook time: 43 minutes | Serves 4

- Spice Rub:
- 2 tablespoons brown sugar
- 2 tablespoons paprika
- 1 teaspoon dry mustard powder
- 1 teaspoon chilli powder
- 2 tablespoons coarse sea salt or kosher salt
- 2 teaspoons coarsely ground black pepper
- 1 tablespoon vegetable oil
- 1 (1.6 kg) chicken, cut into 8 pieces

1. Prepare Spice Rub: In a bowl, combine brown sugar, paprika, mustard powder, chilli powder, salt, and pepper to make the spice rub. 2. Coat Chicken: Rub olive oil all over the chicken pieces. Then, rub the spice mix onto the chicken, ensuring they are completely covered. This can be done in a zipper sealable bag. Marinate the chicken in the refrigerator if desired. 3. Preheat Air Fryer: Preheat the air fryer to 190ºC (375ºF). 4. Cook Chicken: Place chicken thighs and drumsticks into the zone 1 and zone 2 air fryer basket. Select zone 1, select ROAST, set temperature to190ºC, set time to 10 minutes. Press MATCH COOK to match zone 2 setting to zone 1. Then, press START/PAUSE to begin. Flip the chicken pieces and air fry for another 10 minutes. Remove and let them rest on a plate. Air fry the chicken breasts, skin side down, for 8 minutes. Flip and air fry for another 12 minutes. 5. Rest and Serve: Let the chicken rest for 5 minutes before serving. Serve warm with mashed potatoes and a green salad or vegetables.

Indian Fennel Chicken

Prep time: 30 minutes | Cook time: 15 minutes | Serves 4

- 450 g boneless, skinless chicken thighs, cut crosswise into thirds
- 1 brown onion, cut into 1½-inch-thick slices
- 1 tablespoon coconut oil, melted
- 2 teaspoons minced fresh ginger
- 2 teaspoons minced garlic
- 1 teaspoon smoked paprika
- 1 teaspoon ground fennel
- 1 teaspoon garam masala
- 1 teaspoon ground turmeric
- 1 teaspoon kosher salt
- ½ to 1 teaspoon cayenne pepper
- Vegetable oil spray
- 2 teaspoons fresh lemon juice
- 5 g chopped fresh coriander or parsley

1. Prepare Chicken: Use a fork to pierce the chicken breasts all over to allow the marinade to penetrate better. 2. Marinate Chicken: In a large bowl, combine sliced onion, melted coconut oil, grated ginger, minced garlic, paprika, fennel seeds, garam masala, turmeric, salt, and cayenne pepper. Add the chicken breasts to the bowl, toss to combine, and marinate at room temperature for 30 minutes, or cover and refrigerate for up to 24 hours. 3. Preheat Air Fryer: Preheat the air fryer to 180ºC (350ºF). 4. Cook Chicken: Place the marinated chicken and onion slices in the zone 1 and zone 2 air fryer baskets, discarding any remaining marinade. Spray with vegetable oil spray. Select zone 1, select ROAST, set temperature to180ºC, set time to 15 minutes. Press MATCH COOK to match zone 2 setting to zone 1. Then, press START/PAUSE to begin. Halfway through the cooking time, remove the basket, spray the chicken and onion with more vegetable oil spray, and toss gently to coat. Use a meat thermometer to ensure the chicken has reached an internal temperature of 76ºC (170ºF). 5. Serve: Transfer the cooked chicken and onion to a serving platter. Sprinkle with fresh lemon juice and chopped coriander before serving.

Bruschetta Chicken

Prep time: 10 minutes | Cook time: 20 minutes | Serves 4

Bruschetta Stuffing:
- 1 tomato, diced
- 3 tablespoons balsamic vinegar
- 1 teaspoon Italian seasoning
- 2 tablespoons chopped fresh basil
- 3 garlic cloves, minced
- 2 tablespoons extra-virgin olive oil

Chicken:
- 4 (115 g) boneless, skinless chicken breasts, cut 4 slits each
- 1 teaspoon Italian seasoning
- Chicken seasoning or rub, to taste
- Cooking spray

1. Preheat the air fryer to 190 ºC. Spritz the zone 1 and zone 2 air fryer basket with cooking spray. 2. Combine the ingredients for the bruschetta stuffing in a bowl. Stir to mix well. Set aside. 3. Rub the chicken breasts with Italian seasoning and chicken seasoning on a clean work surface. 4. Arrange the chicken breasts, slits side up, in a single layer in the zone 1 and zone 2 air fryer baskets and spritz with cooking spray. 5. Select zone 1, Select ROAST, Set temperature to 190 ºC, set time to 7 minutes. Press MATCH COOK to match zone 2 setting to zone 1. Then, press START/PAUSE to begin. 6. Then open the air fryer and fill the slits in the chicken with the bruschetta stuffing. Cook for another 3 minutes or until the chicken is well browned. 7. Serve immediately.

Ham Chicken with Cheese

Prep time: 15 minutes | Cook time: 25 minutes | Serves 4

- 55 g unsalted butter, softened
- 115 g cream cheese, softened
- 1½ teaspoons Dijon mustard
- 2 tablespoons white wine vinegar
- 60 ml water
- 280 g shredded cooked chicken
- 115 g gammon, chopped
- 115 g sliced Swiss or Provolone cheese

1. Preheat the air fryer to 190ºC. Lightly coat a casserole dish that will fit in the air fryer, such as an 8-inch round pan, with olive oil and set aside. 2. In a large bowl and using an electric mixer, combine the butter, cream cheese, Dijon mustard, and vinegar. With the motor running at low speed, slowly add the water and beat until smooth. Set aside. 3. Arrange an even layer of chicken in the bottom of the prepared pan for zone 1, followed by the gammon. Spread the butter and cream cheese mixture on top of the gammon, followed by the cheese slices on the top layer. Select zone 1, Select ROAST, Set temperature to 190ºC, set time to 20-25 minutes. Then, press START/PAUSE to begin until warmed through and the cheese has browned.

Fiesta Chicken Plate

Prep time: 15 minutes | Cook time: 12 to 15 minutes | Serves 4

- 450 g boneless, skinless chicken breasts (2 large breasts)
- 2 tablespoons lime juice
- 1 teaspoon cumin
- ½ teaspoon salt
- 40 g grated Pepper Jack cheese
- 1 (455 g) tin refried beans
- 130 g salsa
- 30 g shredded lettuce
- 1 medium tomato, chopped
- 2 avocados, peeled and sliced
- 1 small onion, sliced into thin rings
- Sour cream
- maize wrap crisps (optional)

1. Split each chicken breast in half lengthwise. 2. Mix lime juice, cumin, and salt together and brush on all surfaces of chicken breasts. 3. Place in zone 1 and zone 2 air fryer basket. Select zone 1, Select ROAST, Set temperature to 200ºC, set time to 12-15 minutes. Press MATCH COOK to match zone 2 setting to zone 1. Then, press START/PAUSE to begin until well done. 4. Divide the cheese evenly over chicken breasts and cook for an additional minute to melt cheese. 5. While chicken is cooking, heat refried beans on stovetop or in microwave. 6. When ready to serve, divide beans among 4 plates. Place chicken breasts on top of beans and spoon salsa over. Arrange the lettuce, tomatoes, and avocados artfully on each plate and scatter with the onion rings. 7. Pass sour cream at the table and serve with maize wrap crisps if desired.

Chipotle Aioli Wings

Prep time: 5 minutes | Cook time: 25 minutes | Serves 6

- 900 g bone-in chicken wings
- ½ teaspoon salt
- ¼ teaspoon ground black pepper
- 2 tablespoons mayonnaise
- 2 teaspoons chipotle powder
- 2 tablespoons lemon juice

1. In a large bowl, toss wings in salt and pepper, then place into ungreased zone 1 and zone 2 air fryer baskets. 2. Select zone 1, Select ROAST, Set temperature to 200 ºC, set time to 25 minutes. Press MATCH COOK to match zone 2 setting to zone 1. Then, press START/PAUSE to begin. Shaking the basket twice while cooking. Wings will be done when golden and have an internal temperature of at least 76ºC. 3. In a small bowl, whisk together mayonnaise, chipotle powder, and lemon juice. Place cooked wings into a large serving bowl and drizzle with aioli. Toss to coat. Serve warm.

Broccoli Cheese Chicken

Prep time: 15 minutes | Cook time: 25 minutes | Serves 4

- 1 tablespoon avocado oil
- 15 g chopped onion
- 35 g finely chopped broccoli
- 115 g cream cheese, at room temperature
- 60 g Cheddar cheese, shredded
- 1 teaspoon garlic powder
- ½ teaspoon sea salt, plus additional for seasoning, divided
- ¼ freshly ground black pepper, plus additional for seasoning, divided
- 900 g boneless, skinless chicken breasts
- 1 teaspoon smoked paprika

1. Heat a medium frying pan over medium-high heat and pour in the avocado oil. Add the onion and broccoli and cook, stirring occasionally, for 5 to 8 minutes, until the onion is tender. 2. Transfer to a large bowl and stir in the cream cheese, Cheddar cheese, and garlic powder, and season to taste with salt and pepper. 3. Hold a sharp knife parallel to the chicken breast and cut a long pocket into one side. Stuff the chicken pockets with the broccoli mixture, using toothpicks to secure the pockets around the filling. 4. In a small dish, combine the paprika, ½ teaspoon salt, and ¼ teaspoon pepper. Sprinkle this over the outside of the chicken. 5. Place the chicken in a single layer in the zone 1 and zone 2 air fryer baskets. 6. Select zone 1, Select ROAST, Set temperature to 200 °C, set time to 14-16 minutes. Press MATCH COOK to match zone 2 setting to zone 1. Then, press START/PAUSE to begin until an instant-read thermometer reads 70°C. Place the chicken on a plate and tent a piece of aluminium foil over the chicken. Allow to rest for 5 to 10 minutes before serving.

Yellow Curry Chicken Thighs with Peanuts

Prep time: 10 minutes | Cook time: 20 minutes | Serves 6

- 120 ml unsweetened full-fat coconut milk
- 2 tablespoons yellow curry paste
- 1 tablespoon minced fresh ginger
- 1 tablespoon minced garlic
- 1 teaspoon kosher salt
- 450 g boneless, skinless chicken thighs, halved crosswise
- 2 tablespoons chopped peanuts

1. In a large bowl, stir together the coconut milk, curry paste, ginger, garlic, and salt until well blended. Add the chicken; toss well to coat. Marinate at room temperature for 30 minutes, or cover and refrigerate for up to 24 hours. 2. Preheat the air fryer to 190°C. 3. Place the chicken (along with marinade) in the baking pans. Place the pan in the zone 1 and zone 2 air fryer baskets. 4. Select zone 1, select ROAST, set temperature to 190°C, set time to 20 minutes. Press MATCH COOK to match zone 2 setting to zone 1. Then, press START/PAUSE to begin. Turning the chicken halfway through the cooking time. Use a meat thermometer to ensure the chicken has reached an internal temperature of 76°C. 5. Sprinkle the chicken with the chopped peanuts and serve.

Cornish Hens with Honey-Lime Glaze

Prep time: 15 minutes | Cook time: 25 to 30 minutes | Serves 2 to 3

- 1 small chicken (680 to 900 g)
- 1 tablespoon honey
- 1 tablespoon lime juice
- 1 teaspoon poultry seasoning
- Salt and pepper, to taste
- Cooking spray

1. To split the chicken into halves, cut through breast bone and down one side of the backbone. 2. Mix the honey, lime juice, and poultry seasoning together and brush or rub onto all sides of the chicken. Season to taste with salt and pepper. 3. Spray the zone 1 and zone 2 air fryer baskets with cooking spray and place hen halves in the baskets, skin-side down. 4. Select zone 1, select ROAST, set temperature to 170°C, set time to 25-30 minutes. Press MATCH COOK to match zone 2 setting to zone 1. Then, press START/PAUSE to begin. 5. Chicken will be done when juices run clear when pierced at leg joint with a fork. Let chicken rest for 5 to 10 minutes before cutting.

Apricot-Glazed Turkey Tenderloin

Prep time: 20 minutes | Cook time: 30 minutes | Serves 4

- Olive oil
- 80 g sugar-free apricot preserves
- ½ tablespoon spicy brown mustard
- 680 g turkey breast tenderloin
- Salt and freshly ground black pepper, to taste

1. Spray the zone 1 air fryer basket lightly with olive oil. 2. In a small bowl, combine the apricot preserves and mustard to make a paste. 3. Season the turkey with salt and pepper. Spread the apricot paste all over the turkey. 4. Place the turkey in the zone 1 air fryer basket and lightly spray with olive oil. 5. Select zone 1, Select ROAST, Set temperature to 190°C, set time to 15 minutes. Then, press START/PAUSE to begin. 6. Flip the turkey over and lightly spray with olive oil. Air fry until the internal temperature reaches at least 80°C for an additional 10 to 15 minutes. 7. Let the turkey rest for 10 minutes before slicing and serving.

Barbecue Chicken and Coleslaw Tostadas

Prep time: 15 minutes | Cook time: 40 minutes | Makes 4 tostadas

Coleslaw:
- 60 g sour cream
- 25 g small green cabbage, finely chopped
- ½ tablespoon white vinegar
- ½ teaspoon garlic powder
- ½ teaspoon salt
- ¼ teaspoon ground black pepper

Tostadas:
- 280 g pulled rotisserie chicken
- 120 ml barbecue sauce
- 4 maize wraps
- 110 g shredded Mozzarella cheese
- Cooking spray

1. Combine the ingredients for the coleslaw in a large bowl. Toss to mix well. 2. Refrigerate until ready to serve. 3. Preheat the air fryer to 190ºC. Spritz the zone 1 and zone 2 air fryer baskets with cooking spray. 4. Toss the chicken with barbecue sauce in a separate large bowl to combine well. Set aside. 5. Place one tortilla in the preheated air fryer and spritz with cooking spray. 6. Select zone 1, select ROAST, set temperature to190ºC, set time to 5 minutes. Press MATCH COOK to match zone 2 setting to zone 1. Then, press START/PAUSE to begin until lightly browned, then spread a quarter of the barbecue chicken and cheese over. 7. Air fry for another 5 minutes or until the cheese melts. 8. Serve the tostadas with coleslaw on top.

Lemon Thyme Roasted Chicken

Prep time: 10 minutes | Cook time: 60 minutes | Serves 6

- 2 tablespoons baking powder
- 1 teaspoon smoked paprika
- Sea salt and freshly ground black pepper, to taste
- 900 g chicken wings or chicken drumettes
- Avocado oil spray
- 80 ml avocado oil
- 120 ml Buffalo hot sauce, such as Frank's RedHot
- 4 tablespoons unsalted butter
- 2 tablespoons apple cider vinegar
- 1 teaspoon minced garlic

1. In a large bowl, stir together the baking powder, smoked paprika, and salt and pepper to taste. Add the chicken wings and toss to coat. 2. Set the air fryer to 200ºC. Spray the wings with oil. 3. Place the wings in the zone 1 and zone 2 baskets in a single layer. 4. Select zone 1, select ROAST, set temperature to 200ºC, set time to 20-25 minutes. Press MATCH COOK to match zone 2 setting to zone 1. Then, press START/PAUSE to begin. Check with an instant-read thermometer and remove when they reach 70ºC. Let rest until they reach 76ºC. 5. While the wings are cooking, whisk together the avocado oil, hot sauce, butter, vinegar, and garlic in a small saucepan over medium-low heat until warm. 6. When the wings are done cooking, toss them with the Buffalo sauce. Serve warm.

Chicken with Bacon and Tomato

Prep time: 25 minutes | Cook time: 10 minutes | Serves 4

- 4 medium-sized skin-on chicken drumsticks
- 1½ teaspoons herbs de Provence
- Salt and pepper, to taste
- 1 tablespoon rice vinegar
- 2 tablespoons olive oil
- 2 garlic cloves, crushed
- 340 g crushed canned tomatoes
- 1 small-size leek, thinly sliced
- 2 slices smoked bacon, chopped

1. Sprinkle the chicken drumsticks with herbs de Provence, salt and pepper; then, drizzle them with rice vinegar and olive oil. Arrange them on zone 1 and zone 2 baskets. 2. Select zone 1, select ROAST, set temperature to180ºC, set time to 8-10 minutes. Press MATCH COOK to match zone 2 setting to zone 1. Then, press START/PAUSE to begin. 3. Press the START/PAUSE button to pause the air fryer; stir in the remaining ingredients and continue to cook for 15 minutes longer; make sure to check them periodically. Bon appétit!

Chicken Legs with Leeks

Prep time: 30 minutes | Cook time: 18 minutes | Serves 6

- 2 leeks, sliced
- 2 large-sized tomatoes, chopped
- 3 cloves garlic, minced
- ½ teaspoon dried oregano
- 6 chicken legs, boneless and skinless
- ½ teaspoon smoked cayenne pepper
- 2 tablespoons olive oil
- A freshly ground nutmeg

1. In a mixing dish, thoroughly combine all ingredients, minus the leeks. Place in the refrigerator and let it marinate overnight. 2. Lay the leeks onto the bottom of the air fryer basket. Top with the chicken legs. 3. Arrange the chicken legs on zone 1 and zone 2 baskets. 4. Select zone 1, select ROAST, set temperature to190ºC, set time to 18 minutes. Press MATCH COOK to match zone 2 setting to zone 1. Then, press START/PAUSE to begin. Turning halfway through. Serve with hoisin sauce.

Chapter 6 Poultry

Chicken Parmesan

Prep time: 15 minutes | Cook time: 10 minutes | Serves 4

- Oil, for spraying
- 2 (230 g) boneless, skinless chicken breasts
- 60 g Italian-style bread crumbs
- 20 g grated Parmesan cheese, plus 45 g shredded
- 4 tablespoons unsalted butter, melted
- 115 g marinara sauce

1. Preheat the air fryer to 180°C. Line the zone 1 and zone 2 air fryer baskets with parchment and spray lightly with oil. 2. Cut each chicken breast in half through its thickness to make 4 thin cutlets. Using a meat tenderizer, pound each cutlet until it is about ¾ inch thick. 3. On a plate, mix together the bread crumbs and grated Parmesan cheese. 4. Lightly brush the chicken with the melted butter, then dip into the bread crumb mixture. 5. Place the chicken in the prepared baskets and spray lightly with oil. 6. Select zone 1, select ROAST, set temperature to 180°C, set time to 6 minutes. Press MATCH COOK to match zone 2 setting to zone 1. Then, press START/PAUSE to begin. Top the chicken with the marinara and shredded Parmesan cheese, dividing evenly. Cook for another 3 to 4 minutes, or until golden brown, crispy, and the internal temperature reaches 76°C.

Bacon Lovers' Stuffed Chicken

Prep time: 15 minutes | Cook time: 10 minutes | Serves 4

- 4 (140 g) boneless, skinless chicken breasts, pounded to ¼ inch thick
- 2 (150 g) packages Boursin cheese (or Kite Hill brand chive cream cheese style spread, softened, for dairy-free)
- 8 slices thin-cut bacon or beef bacon
- Sprig of fresh coriander, for garnish (optional)

1. Spray the zone 1 and zone 2 air fryer baskets with avocado oil. Preheat the air fryer to 200°C. 2. Place one of the chicken breasts on a cutting board. With a sharp knife held parallel to the cutting board, make a 1-inch-wide incision at the top of the breast. Carefully cut into the breast to form a large pocket, leaving a ½-inch border along the sides and bottom. Repeat with the other 3 chicken breasts. 3. Snip the corner of a large resealable plastic bag to form a ¾-inch hole. Place the Boursin cheese in the bag and pipe the cheese into the pockets in the chicken breasts, dividing the cheese evenly among them. 4. Wrap 2 slices of bacon around each chicken breast and secure the ends with toothpicks. 5. Place the bacon-wrapped chicken in the zone 1 and zone 2 air fryer basket. Select zone 1, select ROAST, set temperature to 200°C, set time to 18-20 minutes. Press MATCH COOK to match zone 2 setting to zone 1. Then, press START/PAUSE to begin. 6. After 10 minutes, press START/PAUSE to pause the air fryer. Then, flip them. Press START/PAUSE to continue. Garnish with a sprig of coriander before serving, if desired. 7. Store leftovers in an airtight container in the refrigerator for up to 4 days. Reheat in a preheated 200°C air fryer for 5 minutes, or until warmed through.

Nice Goulash

Prep time: 5 minutes | Cook time: 17 minutes | Serves 2

- 2 red peppers, chopped
- 450 g chicken mince
- 2 medium tomatoes, diced
- 120 ml chicken broth
- Salt and ground black pepper, to taste
- Cooking spray

1. Preheat the air fryer to 186°C. Spritz the zone 1 baking pan with cooking spray. 2. Set the pepper in the baking pan and put in the air fry. Select zone 1, select ROAST, set temperature to 186°C, set time to 5 minutes. Then, press START/PAUSE to begin until the pepper is tender. Shake the basket halfway through. 3. Add the chicken mince and diced tomatoes in the baking pan and stir to mix well. Select zone 1, select ROAST, set temperature to 186°C, set time to 6 minutes. Then, press START/PAUSE to continue until the chicken is lightly browned. 4. Pour the chicken broth over and sprinkle with salt and ground black pepper. Stir to mix well. Broil for an additional 6 minutes. 5. Serve immediately.

Chipotle Drumsticks

Prep time: 15 minutes | Cook time: 20 minutes | Serves 4

- 1 tablespoon tomato paste
- ½ teaspoon chipotle powder
- ¼ teaspoon apple cider vinegar
- ¼ teaspoon garlic powder
- 8 chicken drumsticks
- ½ teaspoon salt
- ⅛ teaspoon ground black pepper

1. In a small bowl, combine tomato paste, chipotle powder, vinegar, and garlic powder. 2. Sprinkle drumsticks with salt and pepper, then place into a large bowl and pour in tomato paste mixture. Toss or stir to evenly coat all drumsticks in mixture. 3. Place drumsticks into ungreased zone 1 and zone 2 air fryer baskets. 4. Select zone 1, select ROAST, set temperature to 200°C, set time to 25 minutes. Press MATCH COOK to match zone 2 setting to zone 1. Then, press START/PAUSE to begin. Turning drumsticks halfway through cooking. Drumsticks will be dark red with an internal temperature of at least 76°C when done. Serve warm.

Golden Chicken Cutlets

Prep time: 15 minutes | Cook time: 15 minutes | Serves 4

- 2 tablespoons panko breadcrumbs
- 20 g grated Parmesan cheese
- ⅛ tablespoon paprika
- ½ tablespoon garlic powder
- 2 large eggs
- 4 chicken cutlets
- 1 tablespoon parsley
- Salt and ground black pepper, to taste
- Cooking spray

1. Preheat air fryer to 200ºC. Spritz the zone 1 and zone 2 air fryer baskets with cooking spray. 2. Combine the breadcrumbs, Parmesan, paprika, garlic powder, salt, and ground black pepper in a large bowl. Stir to mix well. Beat the eggs in a separate bowl. 3. Dredge the chicken cutlets in the beaten eggs, then roll over the breadcrumbs mixture to coat well. Shake the excess off. 4. Transfer the chicken cutlets in the preheated air fryer and spritz with cooking spray. 5. Select zone 1, select ROAST, set temperature to 200ºC, set time to 15 minutes. Press MATCH COOK to match zone 2 setting to zone 1. Then, press START/PAUSE to begin until crispy and golden brown. Flip the cutlets halfway through. 6. Serve with parsley on top.

Air Fried Chicken Potatoes with Sun-Dried Tomato

Prep time: 15 minutes | Cook time: 25 minutes | Serves 2

- 2 teaspoons minced fresh oregano, divided
- 2 teaspoons minced fresh thyme, divided
- 2 teaspoons extra-virgin olive oil, plus extra as needed
- 450 g fingerling potatoes, unpeeled
- 2 (340 g) bone-in split chicken breasts, trimmed
- 1 garlic clove, minced
- 15 g oil-packed sun-dried tomatoes, patted dry and chopped
- 1½ tablespoons red wine vinegar
- 1 tablespoon capers, rinsed and minced
- 1 small shallot, minced
- Salt and ground black pepper, to taste

1. Preheat the air fryer to 180ºC. 2. Combine 1 teaspoon of oregano, 1 teaspoon of thyme, ¼ teaspoon of salt, ¼ teaspoon of ground black pepper, 1 teaspoons of olive oil in a large bowl. Add the potatoes and toss to coat well. 3. Combine the chicken with remaining thyme, oregano, and olive oil. Sprinkle with garlic, salt, and pepper. Toss to coat well. 4. Place the potatoes in the preheated zone 1 air fryer, then arrange the chicken on top of the potatoes. 5. Select zone 1, select ROAST, set temperature 180ºC, set time to 25 minutes. Then, press START/PAUSE to begin until the internal temperature of the chicken reaches at least 76ºC and the potatoes are wilted. Flip the chicken and potatoes halfway through. 6. Meanwhile, combine the sun-dried tomatoes, vinegar, capers, and shallot in a separate large bowl. Sprinkle with salt and ground black pepper. Toss to mix well. 7. Remove the chicken and potatoes from the air fryer and allow to cool for 10 minutes. Serve with the sun-dried tomato mix.

Lemon-Basil Turkey Breasts

Prep time: 30 minutes | Cook time: 58 minutes | Serves 4

- 2 tablespoons olive oil
- 900 g turkey breasts, bone-in, skin-on
- Coarse sea salt and ground black pepper, to taste
- 1 teaspoon fresh basil leaves, chopped
- 2 tablespoons lemon zest, grated

1. Rub olive oil on all sides of the turkey breasts; sprinkle with salt, pepper, basil, and lemon zest. 2. Place the turkey breasts skin side up on the parchment-lined zone 1 and zone 2 air fryer baskets. 3. Select zone 1, select ROAST, set temperature to 170ºC, set time to 30 minutes. Press MATCH COOK to match zone 2 setting to zone 1. Then, press START/PAUSE to begin. Now, turn them over and cook an additional 28 minutes. 4. Serve with lemon wedges, if desired. Bon appétit!

Potato-Crusted Chicken

Prep time: 15 minutes | Cook time: 22 to 25 minutes | Serves 4

- 60 g buttermilk
- 1 large egg, beaten
- 180 g instant potato flakes
- 20 g grated Parmesan cheese
- 1 teaspoon salt
- ½ teaspoon freshly ground black pepper
- 2 whole boneless, skinless chicken breasts (about 450 g each), halved
- 1 to 2 tablespoons oil

1. In a shallow bowl, whisk the buttermilk and egg until blended. In another shallow bowl, stir together the potato flakes, cheese, salt, and pepper. 2. One at a time, dip the chicken pieces in the buttermilk mixture and the potato flake mixture, coating thoroughly. 3. Preheat the air fryer to 200ºC. Line the zone 1 and zone 2 air fryer baskets with parchment paper. 4. Place the coated chicken on the parchment and spritz with oil. 5. Select zone 1, select ROAST, set temperature to 200ºC, set time to 15 minutes. Press MATCH COOK to match zone 2 setting to zone 1. Then, press START/PAUSE to begin. Flip the chicken, spritz it with oil, and cook for 7 to 10 minutes more until the outside is crispy and the inside is no longer pink.

Chicken Hand Pies

Prep time: 30 minutes | Cook time: 10 minutes per batch | Makes 8 pies

- 180 ml chicken broth
- 130 g frozen mixed peas and carrots
- 140 g cooked chicken, chopped
- 1 tablespoon cornflour
- 1 tablespoon milk
- Salt and pepper, to taste
- 1 (8-count) tin organic flaky biscuits
- Oil for misting or cooking spray

1. In a medium saucepan, bring chicken broth to a boil. Stir in the frozen peas and carrots and cook for 5 minutes over medium heat. Stir in chicken. 2. Mix the cornflour into the milk until it dissolves. Stir it into the simmering chicken broth mixture and cook just until thickened. 3. Remove from heat, add salt and pepper to taste, and let cool slightly. 4. Lay biscuits out on wax paper. Peel each biscuit apart in the middle to make 2 rounds so you have 16 rounds total. Using your hands or a rolling pin, flatten each biscuit round slightly to make it larger and thinner. 5. Divide chicken filling among 8 of the biscuit rounds. Place remaining biscuit rounds on top and press edges all around. Use the tines of a fork to crimp biscuit edges and make sure they are sealed well. 6. Spray both sides lightly with oil or cooking spray. 7. Cook in a single layer, arrange them on zone 1 and zone 2 baskets. Select zone 1, select ROAST, set temperature to 170ºC, set time to 10 minutes. Press MATCH COOK to match zone 2 setting to zone 1. Then, press START/PAUSE to begin until biscuit dough is cooked through and golden brown.

Mediterranean Stuffed Chicken Breasts

Prep time: 5 minutes | Cook time: 20 to 25 minutes | Serves 4

- 4 small boneless, skinless chicken breast halves (about 680 g)
- Salt and freshly ground black pepper, to taste
- 115 g goat cheese
- 6 pitted Kalamata olives, coarsely chopped
- Zest of ½ lemon
- 1 teaspoon minced fresh rosemary or ½ teaspoon ground dried rosemary
- 25 g ground almonds
- 60 ml balsamic vinegar
- 6 tablespoons unsalted butter

1. Preheat the air fryer to 180ºC. 2. With a boning knife, cut a wide pocket into the thickest part of each chicken breast half, taking care not to cut all the way through. Season the chicken evenly on both sides with salt and freshly ground black pepper. 3. In a small bowl, mix the cheese, olives, lemon zest, and rosemary. Stuff the pockets with the cheese mixture and secure with toothpicks. 4. Place the ground almonds in a shallow bowl and dredge the chicken, shaking off the excess. Coat lightly with olive oil spray. 5. Working in batches if necessary, arrange the chicken breasts in a single layer in the air fryer basket. Pausing halfway through the cooking time to flip the chicken, air fry for 20 to 25 minutes, until a thermometer inserted into the thickest part registers 76ºC. 6. While the chicken is baking, prepare the sauce. In a small pan over medium heat, simmer the balsamic vinegar until thick and syrupy, about 5 minutes. Set aside until the chicken is done. When ready to serve, warm the sauce over medium heat and whisk in the butter, 1 tablespoon at a time, until melted and smooth. Season to taste with salt and pepper. 7. Serve the chicken breasts with the sauce drizzled on top.

Teriyaki Chicken Thighs with Lemony Mangetouts

Prep time: 30 minutes | Cook time: 34 minutes | Serves 4

- 60 ml chicken broth
- ½ teaspoon grated fresh ginger
- ⅛ teaspoon red pepper flakes
- 1½ tablespoons soy sauce
- 4 (140 g) bone-in chicken thighs, trimmed
- 1 tablespoon mirin
- ½ teaspoon cornflour
- 1 tablespoon sugar
- 170 g mangetout, strings removed
- ⅛ teaspoon lemon zest
- 1 garlic clove, minced
- ¼ teaspoon salt
- Ground black pepper, to taste
- ½ teaspoon lemon juice

1. Prepare Chicken Marinade: In a large bowl, combine chicken broth, grated ginger, red pepper flakes, and soy sauce. Stir well to mix. 2. Marinate Chicken: Pierce holes into the chicken skin. Add chicken to the marinade mixture and toss to coat. Let it sit for 10 minutes to marinate. 3. Preheat Air Fryer: Preheat the air fryer to 206ºC. 4. Prepare Marinade Glaze: Transfer 2 tablespoons of marinade to a microwave-safe bowl. Add mirin, cornflour, and sugar. Stir well and microwave for 1 minute until thickened. Set aside. 5. Cook Chicken: Pat dry the marinated chicken with paper towels. Arrange chicken in the zone 1 and zone 2 air fryer baskets, skin side up. Select zone 1, Select ROAST, Set temperature to 206ºC, set time to 25 minutes. Press MATCH COOK to match zone 2 setting to zone 1. Then, press START/PAUSE to begin. until internal temperature reaches 76ºC (170ºF), flipping halfway through. 6. Glaze Chicken: Brush chicken skin with marinade glaze. Air fry for an additional 5 minutes or until glazed. 7. Prepare Lemon Mangetouts: While chicken is cooking, combine reserved chicken fat, mangetouts, lemon zest, minced garlic, salt, and pepper in a bowl. Toss well to coat. 8. Cook Lemon Mangetouts: Transfer mangetouts to the zone 1 and zone 2 air fryer baskets and air fry for 3 minutes or until soft. 9. Serve: Remove mangetouts from the air fryer and toss with lemon juice. Serve chicken with lemon mangetouts on the side.

Breaded Turkey Cutlets

Prep time: 5 minutes | Cook time: 8 minutes | Serves 4

- 30 g whole wheat bread crumbs
- ¼ teaspoon paprika
- ¼ teaspoon salt
- ¼ teaspoon black pepper
- ⅛ teaspoon dried sage
- ⅛ teaspoon garlic powder
- 1 egg
- 4 turkey breast cutlets
- Chopped fresh parsley, for serving

1. Preheat the air fryer to 192°C. 2. In a medium shallow bowl, whisk together the bread crumbs, paprika, salt, black pepper, sage, and garlic powder. 3. In a separate medium shallow bowl, whisk the egg until frothy. 4. Dip each turkey cutlet into the egg mixture, then into the bread crumb mixture, coating the outside with the crumbs. Place the breaded turkey cutlets in a single layer in the bottom of the zone 1 and zone 2 air fryer baskets, making sure that they don't touch each other. 5. Select zone 1, select ROAST, set temperature to192°C, set time to 5 minutes. Press MATCH COOK to match zone 2 setting to zone 1. Then, press START/PAUSE to begin. Turn the cutlets over, then bake for 4 minutes more, or until the internal temperature reaches 76°C. Sprinkle on the parsley and serve.

Chicken with Pineapple and Peach

Prep time: 10 minutes | Cook time: 14 to 15 minutes | Serves 4

- 1 (450 g) low-sodium boneless, skinless chicken breasts, cut into 1-inch pieces
- 1 medium red onion, chopped
- 1 (230 g) tin pineapple chunks, drained, 60 ml juice reserved
- 1 tablespoon peanut oil or safflower oil
- 1 peach, peeled, pitted, and cubed
- 1 tablespoon cornflour
- ½ teaspoon ground ginger
- ¼ teaspoon ground allspice
- Brown rice, cooked (optional)

1. Preheat Air Fryer: Preheat the air fryer to 196°C (385°F). 2. Prepare Chicken Stir Fry: In a medium metal bowl, mix the chicken, red onion, pineapple chunks, and peanut oil until well combined. 3. Cook Chicken Mixture: Place the bowl in the preheated zone 1 and zone 2 air fryers. Select zone 1, select ROAST, set temperature to 196°C, set time to 9 minutes. Press MATCH COOK to match zone 2 setting to zone 1. Then, press START/PAUSE to begin. Remove the bowl and stir the mixture. 4. Add Peach: Add the sliced peach to the chicken mixture and return the bowl to the air fryer. Bake for an additional 3 minutes. 5. Prepare Sauce: In a small bowl, whisk together the reserved pineapple juice, cornflour, grated ginger, and allspice until smooth. 6. Add Sauce: Pour the prepared sauce over the chicken mixture and stir to combine. 7. Finish Cooking: Bake for 2 to 3 more minutes, or until the chicken reaches an internal temperature of 76°C (170°F) and the sauce is slightly thickened. 8. Serve: Serve the Hawaiian chicken stir fry immediately over hot cooked brown rice, if desired.

Almond-Crusted Chicken

Prep time: 15 minutes | Cook time: 25 minutes | Serves 4

- 20 g slivered almonds
- 2 (170 g) boneless, skinless chicken breasts
- 2 tablespoons full-fat mayonnaise
- 1 tablespoon Dijon mustard

1. Pulse the almonds in a food processor or chop until finely chopped. Place almonds evenly on a plate and set aside. 2. Completely slice each chicken breast in half lengthwise. 3. Mix the mayonnaise and mustard in a small bowl and then coat chicken with the mixture. 4. Lay each piece of chicken in the chopped almonds to fully coat. Carefully move the pieces into the zone 1 and zone 2 air fryer baskets. 5. Select zone 1, select ROAST, set temperature to 180°C, set time to 25 minutes. Press MATCH COOK to match zone 2 setting to zone 1. Then, press START/PAUSE to begin. 6. Chicken will be done when it has reached an internal temperature of 76°C or more. Serve warm.

Thai Curry Meatballs

Prep time: 10 minutes | Cook time: 10 minutes | Serves 4

- 450 g chicken mince
- 15 g chopped fresh coriander
- 1 teaspoon chopped fresh mint
- 1 tablespoon fresh lime juice
- 1 tablespoon Thai red, green, or yellow curry paste
- 1 tablespoon fish sauce
- 2 garlic cloves, minced
- 2 teaspoons minced fresh ginger
- ½ teaspoon kosher salt
- ½ teaspoon black pepper
- ¼ teaspoon red pepper flakes

1. Preheat the air fryer to 200°C. 2. In a large bowl, gently mix the chicken mince, coriander, mint, lime juice, curry paste, fish sauce, garlic, ginger, salt, black pepper, and red pepper flakes until thoroughly combined. 3. Form the mixture into 16 meatballs. Place the meatballs in a single layer in the zone 1 and zone 2 air fryer baskets. 4. Select zone 1, select ROAST, set temperature to 200°C, set time to 10 minutes. Press MATCH COOK to match zone 2 setting to zone 1. Then, press START/PAUSE to begin. Turning the meatballs halfway through the cooking time. Use a meat thermometer to ensure the meatballs have reached an internal temperature of 76°C. Serve immediately.

Chapter 7: Snacks and Starters

Chapter 7 Snacks and Starters

Garlic-Roasted Tomatoes and Olives

Prep time: 5 minutes | Cook time: 20 minutes | Serves 6

- 300 g cherry tomatoes
- 4 garlic cloves, roughly chopped
- ½ red onion, roughly chopped
- 160 g black olives
- 180 g green olives
- 1 tablespoon fresh basil, minced
- 1 tablespoon fresh oregano, minced
- 2 tablespoons olive oil
- ¼ to ½ teaspoon salt

1. Preheat the air fryer to 190ºC. 2. In a large bowl, combine all of the ingredients and toss together so that the tomatoes and olives are coated well with the olive oil and herbs. 3. Pour the mixture into the zone 1 and zone 2 air fryer baskets. Select zone 1, select ROAST, set temperature to 190ºC, set time to 10 minutes. Press MATCH COOK to match zone 2 setting to zone 1. Then, press START/PAUSE to begin. Stir the mixture well, then continue roasting for an additional 10 minutes. 4. Remove from the air fryer, transfer to a serving bowl, and enjoy.

Prawns Egg Rolls

Prep time: 15 minutes | Cook time: 10 minutes per batch | Serves 4

- 1 tablespoon mixed vegetables oil
- ½ head green or savoy cabbage, finely shredded
- 90 g grated carrots
- 240 ml canned bean sprouts, drained
- 1 tablespoon soy sauce
- ½ teaspoon sugar
- 1 teaspoon sesame oil
- 60 ml hoisin sauce
- Freshly ground black pepper, to taste
- 454 g cooked prawns, diced
- 30 g spring onions
- 8 egg roll wrappers (or use spring roll pastry)
- mixed vegetables oil
- Duck sauce

1. Prepare Filling: Preheat a large sauté pan over medium-high heat. Add vegetable oil and sauté cabbage, carrots, and bean sprouts until slightly wilted, about 3 minutes. Add soy sauce, sugar, sesame oil, hoisin sauce, and black pepper. Sauté for a few more minutes. Stir in chopped prawns and spring onions. Cook until vegetables are just tender. Transfer mixture to a colander set over a bowl to cool. Press out any excess water from the filling. 2. Make Egg Rolls: Place egg roll wrappers on a flat surface, with one point facing towards you. Spoon filling onto the center of each wrapper, leaving 2 inches from each corner empty. Brush empty sides of wrapper with water. Fold bottom corner tightly up over the filling, avoiding air pockets. Fold left and right corners towards the center, then tightly roll the egg roll from bottom to top open corner. Press to seal, brushing with extra water if needed. Repeat with remaining wrappers and filling. 3. Preheat Air Fryer: Preheat air fryer to 190ºC (375ºF). 4. Air Fry Egg Rolls: Spray or brush all sides of egg rolls with mixed vegetable oil. Place the egg rolls in zone 1 and zone 1 basket. 5. Select zone 1, select AIR FRY, set temperature to 190ºC, set time to 10 minutes. Press MATCH COOK to match zone 2 setting to zone 1. Then, press START/PAUSE to begin. Turning them over halfway through cooking. 6. Serve: Serve hot with duck sauce or your favorite dipping sauce.

Bruschetta with Basil Pesto

Prep time: 10 minutes | Cook time: 5 to 11 minutes | Serves 4

- 8 slices French bread, ½ inch thick
- 2 tablespoons softened butter
- 120 g shredded mozzarella cheese cheese
- 120 g basil pesto
- 240 g chopped cherry tomatoes
- 2 spring onions, thinly sliced

1. Preheat Air Fryer: Preheat the air fryer to 180ºC (360ºF). 2. Prepare Bread: Spread each slice of bread with butter on one side. Place the bread, butter-side up, in the air fryer basket. Select zone 1, select BAKE, set temperature to 180ºC, set time to 3-5 minutes. Press MATCH COOK to match zone 2 setting to zone 1. Then, press START/PAUSE to begin until the bread is light golden. 3. Add Cheese: Remove the bread from the air fryer and top each piece with shredded cheese. Return the bread to the baskets, bake for 1 to 3 minutes, or until the cheese melts. 4. Prepare Pesto Mixture: In a small bowl, combine the pesto sauce, diced cherry tomatoes, and thinly sliced spring onion. 5. Serve: Once the cheese has melted, remove the bread from the air fryer and place it on a serving plate. Top each slice with some of the pesto mixture. Serve immediately.

Crispy Green Tomato Slices

Prep time: 10 minutes | Cook time: 8 minutes | Makes 12 slices

- 60 g plain flour
- 1 egg
- 120 ml buttermilk
- 120 g cornmeal
- 120 g panko breadcrumbs
- 2 green tomatoes, cut into ¼-inch-thick slices, patted dry
- ½ teaspoon salt
- ½ teaspoon ground black pepper
- Cooking spray

1. Preheat Air Fryer: Preheat the air fryer to 200ºC (390ºF). 2. Prepare Basket: Line the zone 1 and zone 2 air fryer baskets with parchment paper. 3. Prepare Breading Station: Set up three shallow bowls. Pour flour into the first bowl, whisk egg and buttermilk in the second bowl, and combine cornmeal and panko breadcrumbs in the third bowl. 4. Coat Tomato Slices: Dredge tomato slices in flour first, then dip into the egg mixture, and finally coat with the cornmeal mixture. Shake off any excess. 5. Transfer to Air Fryer: Place the well-coated tomato slices in the preheated zone 1 and zone 2 air fryer basket. Sprinkle with salt and ground black pepper, then spritz with cooking spray. 6. Air Fry: Select zone 1, select AIR FRY, set temperature to 200ºC, set time to 8 minutes. Press MATCH COOK to match zone 2 setting to zone 1. Then, press START/PAUSE to begin until crispy and lightly browned, flipping the slices halfway through the cooking time. 7. Serve: Serve the fried green tomatoes immediately as a delicious appetizer or side dish.

Bacon-Wrapped A Pickled Gherkin Spear

Prep time: 10 minutes | Cook time: 8 minutes | Serves 4

- 8 to 12 slices bacon
- 60 g soft white cheese
- 40 g shredded mozzarella cheese cheese
- 8 fresh dill a pickled gherkin spears
- 120 ml ranch dressing

1. Prepare Bacon and Cheese Mixture: Lay the bacon slices on a flat surface. In a medium-sized bowl, combine the soft white cheese and mozzarella cheese. Stir until thoroughly combined. Spread the cheese mixture evenly over the bacon slices. 2. Wrap Pickled Gherkin Spears: Place a pickled gherkin spear on a bacon slice and roll the bacon around the gherkin in a spiral, ensuring the gherkin is fully covered. You may need to use more than one slice of bacon per gherkin to fully cover the spear. Fold in the ends to ensure the bacon stays put. Repeat to wrap all the pickled cucumbers. 3. Preheat Air Fryer: Preheat the air fryer to 200ºC (400ºF). 4. Air Fry: Place the wrapped pickled gherkin spears in the zone 1 and zone 2 air fryer baskets in a single layer. Select zone 1, select AIR FRY, set temperature to 200ºC, set time to 8 minutes. Press MATCH COOK to match zone 2 setting to zone 1. Then, press START/PAUSE to begin or until the bacon is fully cooked and crisp on the edges. 5. Serve: Serve the bacon-wrapped pickled gherkin spears with ranch dressing on the side for dipping.

Herbed Green Lentil Rice Balls

Prep time: 5 minutes | Cook time: 11 minutes | Serves 6

- 120 ml cooked green lentils
- 2 garlic cloves, minced
- ¼ white onion, minced
- 60 ml parsley leaves
- 5 basil leaves
- 235 ml cooked brown rice
- 1 tablespoon lemon juice
- 1 tablespoon olive oil
- ½ teaspoon salt

1. Preheat the air fryer to 192ºC. 2. In a food processor, pulse the cooked lentils with the garlic, onion, parsley, and basil until mostly smooth. (You will want some bits of lentils in the mixture.) Pour the lentil mixture into a large bowl, and stir in brown rice, lemon juice, olive oil, and salt. Stir until well combined. 3. Form the rice mixture into 1-inch balls. 4. Place the rice balls in a single layer in the zone 1 and zone 2 air fryer baskets, making sure that they don't touch each other. 5. Select zone 1, select AIR FRY, set temperature to 192ºC, set time to 6 minutes. Press MATCH COOK to match zone 2 to zone 1. Then, Press START/PAUSE to begin. 6. Turn the rice balls and then fry for an additional 4 to 5 minutes, or until browned on all sides.

Spicy Chicken Bites

Prep time: 10 minutes | Cook time: 10 to 12 minutes | Makes 30 bites

- 227 g boneless and skinless chicken thighs, cut into 30 pieces
- ¼ teaspoon rock salt
- 2 tablespoons hot sauce
- Cooking spray

1. Preheat the air fryer to 200ºC. 2. Spray the zone 1 and zone 2 air fryer baskets with cooking spray and season the chicken bites with the rock salt, then place in the zone 1 and zone 2 baskets. 3. Select zone 1, select ROAST, set temperature to 200ºC, set time to 10-12 minutes. Press MATCH COOK to match zone 2 setting to zone 1. Then, press START/PAUSE to begin. 4. While the chicken bites cook, pour the hot sauce into a large bowl. 5. Remove the bites and add to the sauce bowl, tossing to coat. Serve warm.

Beef and Mango Skewers

Prep time: 10 minutes | Cook time: 4 to 7 minutes | Serves 4

- 340 g beef sirloin tip, cut into 1-inch cubes
- 2 tablespoons balsamic vinegar
- 1 tablespoon olive oil
- 1 tablespoon honey
- ½ teaspoon dried marjoram
- Pinch of salt
- Freshly ground black pepper, to taste
- 1 mango

1. Preheat the air fryer to 200°C. 2. Put the beef cubes in a medium-sized bowl and add the balsamic vinegar, olive oil, honey, marjoram, salt, and pepper. Mix well, then massage the marinade into the beef with your hands. Set aside. 3. To prepare the mango, stand it on end and cut the skin off, using a sharp knife. Then carefully cut around the oval pit to remove the flesh. Cut the mango into 1-inch cubes. 4. Thread metal skewers alternating with three beef cubes and two mango cubes. 5. Roast the skewers in the zone 1 and zone 2 air fryer baskets. Select zone 1, select AIR FRY, set temperature to 200°C, set time to 4-7 minutes. Press MATCH COOK to match zone 2 to zone 1. Then, Press START/PAUSE to begin until the beef is browned and at least 63°C. 6. Serve hot.

Mixed Vegetables Pot Stickers

Prep time: 12 minutes | Cook time: 11 to 18 minutes | Makes 12 pot stickers

- 70 g shredded red cabbage
- 25 g chopped button mushrooms
- 35 g grated carrot
- 2 tablespoons minced onion
- 2 garlic cloves, minced
- 2 teaspoons grated fresh ginger
- 12 gyoza/pot sticker wrappers
- 2½ teaspoons olive oil, divided

1. Prepare Vegetable Filling: In a mixing bowl, combine finely chopped red cabbage, sliced mushrooms, grated carrot, diced onion, minced garlic, and freshly grated ginger. Add a tablespoon of water and toss to combine. 2. Fill the Wrappers: Lay out the pot sticker wrappers on a clean surface. Spoon a tablespoon of the vegetable filling onto each wrapper. Fold the wrapper in half over the filling to create a half-circle shape. Moisten one edge with water and press to seal. 3. Air Fry the Pot Stickers: Heat 1¼ teaspoons of olive oil in a separate pan. Arrange the prepared pot stickers, seam-side up, in the zone 1 and zone 2 pans. Select zone 1, select AIR FRY, set temperature to 190°C, set time to 5 minutes. Press MATCH COOK to match zone 2 to zone 1. Then, Press START/PAUSE to begin until the bottoms are lightly golden. Add a tablespoon of water to the pan and return it to the air fryer. 4. Finish Cooking: Air fry for an additional 4 to 6 minutes until the pot stickers are heated through. Repeat the process with the remaining pot stickers, using the remaining oil and another tablespoon of water. 5. Serve: Once cooked, serve the pot stickers immediately. They pair well with a dipping sauce of your choice and make for a delightful appetizer or snack. Enjoy the crispy texture and flavorful filling!

Lemony Endive in Curried Yoghurt

Prep time: 5 minutes | Cook time: 10 minutes | Serves 6

- 6 heads endive
- 120 ml plain and fat-free yoghurt
- 3 tablespoons lemon juice
- 1 teaspoon garlic powder
- ½ teaspoon curry powder
- Salt and ground black pepper, to taste

1. Wash the endives and slice them in half lengthwise. 2. In a bowl, mix together the yoghurt, lemon juice, garlic powder, curry powder, salt and pepper. 3. Brush the endive halves with the marinade, coating them completely. Allow to sit for at least 30 minutes or up to 24 hours. 4. Preheat the air fryer to 160°C. 5. Put the endives in the zone 1 and zone 2 air fryer baskets. 6. Select zone 1, select AIR FRY, set temperature to 160°C, set time to 10 minutes. Press MATCH COOK to match zone 2 setting to zone 1. Then, press START/PAUSE to begin. 6. Serve hot.

Easy Spiced Nuts

Prep time: 5 minutes | Cook time: 25 minutes | Makes 3 L

- 1 egg white, lightly beaten
- 48 g sugar
- 1 teaspoon salt
- ½ teaspoon cinnamon powder
- ¼ teaspoon ground cloves
- ¼ teaspoon ground allspice
- Pinch ground cayenne pepper
- 100 g pecan halves
- 135 g cashews
- 140 g almonds

1. Combine the egg white with the sugar and spices in a bowl. 2. Preheat the air fryer to 150°C. 3. Spray or brush the air fryer basket with mixed vegetables oil. Toss the nuts together in the spiced egg white and transfer the nuts to the zone 1 and zone 2 air fryer baskets. 4. Select zone 1, select AIR FRY, set temperature to 150°C, set time to 25 minutes. Press MATCH COOK to match zone 2 to zone 1. Then, Press START/PAUSE to begin. Stirring the nuts in the baskets a few times during the cooking process. Taste the nuts (carefully because they will be very hot) to see if they are crunchy and nicely toasted. Air fry for a few more minutes if necessary. 5. Serve warm or cool to at room temperature and store in an airtight container for up to two weeks.

Stuffed Figs with Goat Cheese and Honey

Prep time: 5 minutes | Cook time: 10 minutes | Serves 4

- 8 fresh figs
- 57 g goat cheese
- ¼ teaspoon cinnamon powder
- 1 tablespoon honey, plus more for serving
- 1 tablespoon olive oil

1. Preheat Air Fryer: Preheat the air fryer to 180ºC (360ºF). Line the zone 1 and zone 2 baskets with baking paper, leaving an overhang on the sides for easy removal after cooking. 2. Mix Ingredients: In a large bowl, mix together the rolled oats, honey, peanut butter, dried fruit, chopped nuts, cinnamon, and a pinch of salt until well combined. 3. Press into Pan: Press the oat mixture into the prepared baking dish in zone 1 and zone 2 baskets. 4. Bake: Select zone 1, select BAKE, set temperature to 180ºC, set time to 15 minutes. Press MATCH COOK to match zone 2 setting to zone 1. Then, press START/PAUSE to begin. 5. Remove and Cool: Remove the baking dish from the air fryer and use the edges of the baking paper to lift the muesli cake out of the pan. Allow it to cool for 5 minutes. 6. Slice: After cooling, slice the muesli cake into 6 equal bars. 7. Serve or Store: Serve the bars immediately or wrap them in cling film and store at room temperature for up to 1 week.

Pepperoni Pizza Dip

Prep time: 10 minutes | Cook time: 10 minutes | Serves 6

- 170 g soft white cheese
- 85 g shredded Italian cheese blend
- 60 ml soured cream
- 1½ teaspoons dried Italian seasoning
- ¼ teaspoon garlic salt
- ¼ teaspoon onion powder
- 165 g pizza sauce
- 42 g sliced miniature pepperoni
- 400 g sliced black olives
- 1 tablespoon thinly sliced spring onion
- Cut-up raw mixed vegetables, toasted baguette slices, pitta chips, or tortilla chips, for serving

1. Prepare Cheese Mixture: In a small bowl, combine the soft white cheese, 28g shredded cheese, soured cream, Italian seasoning, garlic salt, and onion powder. Stir until smooth and well blended. 2. Layer the Dip: Spread the cheese mixture evenly in a baking pan. Top with pizza sauce, spreading it to the edges. Sprinkle with the remaining 56g shredded cheese. Arrange the pepperoni slices on top, followed by the black olives and sliced green onion. 3. Air Fry: Place the baking pan in the zone 1 air fryer basket. Select zone 1, Select BAKE, Set temperature to 180ºC, set time to 10 minutes. Then press START/PAUSE to begin until the pepperoni begins to brown on the edges and the cheese is bubbly and lightly browned.

4. Serve: Let the dip stand for 5 minutes before serving. Serve with mixed vegetables, toasted baguette slices, pitta chips, or tortilla chips for dipping.

Air Fried Spicy Olives

Prep time: 10 minutes | Cook time: 5 minutes | Serves 4

- 340 g pitted black extra-large olives
- 30 g plain flour
- 120 g panko breadcrumbs
- 2 teaspoons dried thyme
- 1 teaspoon red pepper flakes
- 1 teaspoon smoked paprika
- 1 egg beaten with 1 tablespoon water
- Vegetable oil for spraying

1. Preheat the air fryer to 200ºC. 2. Drain the olives and place them on a paper towel–lined plate to dry. 3. Put the flour on a plate. 4. Combine the panko, thyme, red pepper flakes, and paprika on a separate plate. 5. Dip an olive in the flour, shaking off any excess, then coat with egg mixture. 6. Dredge the olive in the panko mixture, pressing to make the crumbs adhere, and place the breaded olive on a platter. 7. Repeat with the remaining olives. 8. Spray the olives with oil and place them in a single layer in the zone 1 and zone 2 air fryer baskets. 9. Select zone 1, select AIR FRY, set temperature to 200ºC, set time to 5 minutes. Press MATCH COOK to match zone 2 to zone 1. Then, Press START/PAUSE to begin until the breading is browned and crispy. 10. Serve warm

Crispy Filo Artichoke Triangles

Prep time: 15 minutes | Cook time: 9 to 12 minutes | Makes 18 triangles

- 70 g Ricotta cheese
- 1 egg white
- 60 g minced and drained artichoke hearts
- 3 tablespoons grated mozzarella cheese cheese
- ½ teaspoon dried thyme
- 6 sheets frozen filo pastry, thawed
- 2 tablespoons melted butter

1. Preheat the air fryer to 200ºC. 2. In a small bowl, combine the Ricotta cheese, egg white, artichoke hearts, mozzarella cheese cheese, and thyme, and mix well. 3. Cover the filo pastry with a damp kitchen towel while you work so it doesn't dry out. Using one sheet at a time, place on the work surface and cut into thirds lengthwise. 4. Put about 1½ teaspoons of the filling on each strip at the base. Fold the bottom right-hand tip of phyllo over the filling to meet the other side in a triangle, then continue folding in a triangle. Brush each triangle with butter to seal the edges. Repeat with the remaining phyllo dough and filling. 5. Place the triangles in the zone 1 and zone 1 air fryer baskets. Select zone 1, select BAKE, set temperature to 200ºC, set time to 3-4 minutes. Press MATCH COOK to match zone 2 to zone 1. Then, Press START/PAUSE to begin until the filo is golden and crisp. 6. Serve hot.

Turkey Burger Sliders

Prep time: 10 minutes | Cook time: 5 to 7 minutes | Makes 8 sliders

- 450 g finely chopped turkey
- ¼ teaspoon curry powder
- 1 teaspoon Hoisin sauce
- ½ teaspoon salt
- 8 mini rolls
- 60 g thinly sliced red onions
- 60 g slivered green or red pepper
- 100 g fresh diced pineapple
- Light soft white cheese

1. Combine turkey, curry powder, Hoisin sauce, and salt and mix together well. 2. Shape turkey mixture into 8 small burger patties. 3. Place burger patties in zone 1 and zone 2 air fryer basket. Select zone 1, select AIR FRY, set temperature to 180°C, set time to 5-7 minutes. Press MATCH COOK to match zone 2 to zone 1. Then, Press START/PAUSE to begin until burger patties are well done, and the juices are clear. 4. Place each patty on the bottom half of a slider roll and top with onions, peppers, and pineapple. Spread the remaining bun halves with soft white cheese to taste, place on top, and serve.

Golden Onion Rings

Prep time: 15 minutes | Cook time: 14 minutes per batch | Serves 4

- 1 large white onion, peeled and cut into ½ to ¾-inch-thick slices (about 475 g)
- 120 ml semi-skimmed milk
- 115 g wholemeal pastry flour, or plain flour
- 2 tablespoons cornflour
- ¾ teaspoon sea salt, divided
- ½ teaspoon freshly ground black pepper, divided
- ¾ teaspoon garlic powder, divided
- 110 g wholemeal breadcrumbs, or gluten-free breadcrumbs
- Cooking oil spray (coconut, sunflower, or safflower)
- tomato ketchup, for serving (optional)

1. Carefully separate the onion slices into rings—a gentle touch is important here. 2. Place the milk in a shallow dish and set aside. 3. Make the first breading: In a medium-sized bowl, stir together the flour, cornflour, ¼ teaspoon of salt, ¼ teaspoon of pepper, and ¼ teaspoon of garlic powder. Set aside. 4. Make the second breading: In a separate medium bowl, stir together the breadcrumbs with the remaining ½ teaspoon of salt, the remaining ½ teaspoon of garlic, and the remaining ½ teaspoon of pepper. Set aside. 5. Insert the crisper plate into the zone 1 and zone 2 baskets, and the basket into the units. Preheat the unit by selecting zone 1, selecting AIR FRY, setting the temperature to 200°C, and setting the time to 3 minutes. Press MATCH COOK to match zone 2 setting to zone 1. Select START/PAUSE to begin. 6. Once the unit is preheated, spray the crisper plate and the basket with cooking oil. 7. To make the onion rings, dip one ring into the milk and into the first breading mixture. Dip the ring into the milk again and back into the first breading mixture, coating thoroughly. Dip the ring into the milk one last time and then into the second breading mixture, coating thoroughly. Gently lay the onion ring in the basket. Repeat with additional rings and, as you place them into the basket, do not overlap them too much. Once all the onion rings are in the basket, generously spray the tops with cooking oil.8. Select zone 1, select AIR FRY, set the temperature to 200°C, and set the time to 14 minutes. Press MATCH COOK to match zone 2 setting to zone 1. Insert the two baskets into the unit. Select START/PAUSE to begin. 9. After 4 minutes, open the units and spray the rings generously with cooking oil. Close the two units to resume cooking. After 3 minutes, remove the baskets and spray the onion rings again. Remove the rings, turn them over, and place them back into the baskets. Generously spray them again with oil. Reinsert the baskets to resume cooking. After 4 minutes, generously spray the rings with oil one last time. Resume cooking for the remaining 3 minutes, or until the onion rings are very crunchy and brown. 10. When the cooking is complete, serve the hot rings with tomato ketchup, or other sauce of choice.

Crunchy Basil White Beans

Prep time: 2 minutes | Cook time: 19 minutes | Serves 2

- 1 (425 g) tin cooked white beans
- 2 tablespoons olive oil
- 1 teaspoon fresh sage, chopped
- ¼ teaspoon garlic powder
- ¼ teaspoon salt, divided
- 1 teaspoon chopped fresh basil

1. Preheat the air fryer to 190°C. 2. In a medium-sized bowl, mix together the beans, olive oil, sage, garlic, ⅛ teaspoon salt, and basil. 3. Pour the white beans into the air fryer and spread them out in a single layer. 4. Select zone 1, select BAKE, set temperature to 190°C, set time to 10 minutes. Then, Press START/PAUSE to begin. Stir and continue cooking for an additional 5 to 9 minutes, or until they reach your preferred level of crispiness. 5. Toss with the remaining ⅛ teaspoon salt before serving.

Carrot Chips

Prep time: 15 minutes | Cook time: 8 to 10 minutes | Serves 4

- 1 tablespoon olive oil, plus more for greasing the basket
- 4 to 5 medium carrots, trimmed and thinly sliced
- 1 teaspoon seasoned salt

1. Preheat the air fryer to 200ºC. Grease the zone 1 and zone 2 air fryer baskets with the olive oil. 2. Toss the carrot slices with 1 tablespoon of olive oil and salt in a medium-sized bowl until thoroughly coated. 3. Arrange the carrot slices in the greased zone 1 and zone 2 basket. 4. Select zone 1, select AIR FRY, set temperature to 200ºC, set time to 8-10 minutes. Press MATCH COOK to match zone 2 to zone 1. Then, Press START/PAUSE to begin until the carrot slices are crisp-tender. Shake the basket once during cooking. 5. Transfer the carrot slices to a bowl. 6. Allow to cool for 5 minutes and serve.

Crispy Chilli Chickpeas

Prep time: 5 minutes | Cook time: 15 minutes | Serves 4

- 1 (425 g) tin cooked chickpeas, drained and rinsed
- 1 tablespoon olive oil
- ¼ teaspoon salt
- ⅛ teaspoon chilli powder
- ⅛ teaspoon garlic powder
- ⅛ teaspoon paprika

1. Preheat the air fryer to 190ºC. 2. In a medium-sized bowl, toss all of the ingredients together until the chickpeas are well coated. 3. Pour the chickpeas into the zone 1 and zone 2 air fryer and spread them out in a single layer. 4. Select zone 1, select ROAST, set temperature to 190ºC, set time to 15minutes. Press MATCH COOK to match zone 2 to zone 1. Then, Press START/PAUSE to begin. Stirring once halfway through the cook time.

Chapter 8
Vegetables and Sides

Chapter 8 Vegetables and Sides

Balsamic Brussels Sprouts

Prep time: 5 minutes | Cook time: 12 minutes | Serves 4

- 180 g trimmed and halved fresh Brussels sprouts
- 2 tablespoons olive oil
- ¼ teaspoon salt
- ¼ teaspoon ground black pepper
- 2 tablespoons balsamic vinegar
- 2 slices cooked sugar-free bacon, crumbled

1. In a large bowl, toss Brussels sprouts in olive oil, then sprinkle with salt and pepper. Place into ungreased zone 1 and zone 2 air fryer baskets. 2. Select zone 1, select ROAST, set temperature to 190ºC, set time to 12 minutes. Press MATCH COOK to match zone 2 to zone 1. Then, Press START/PAUSE to begin. Shaking the basket halfway through cooking. Brussels sprouts will be tender and browned when done. 3. Place sprouts in a large serving dish and drizzle with balsamic vinegar. Sprinkle bacon over top. Serve warm.

Banger-Stuffed Mushroom Caps

Prep time: 10 minutes | Cook time: 8 minutes | Serves 2

- 6 large portobello mushroom caps
- 230 g Italian banger
- 15 g chopped onion
- 2 tablespoons blanched finely ground almond flour
- 20 g grated Parmesan cheese
- 1 teaspoon minced fresh garlic

1. Use a spoon to hollow out each mushroom cap, reserving scrapings. 2. In a medium frying pan over medium heat, brown the banger about 10 minutes or until fully cooked and no pink remains. Drain and then add reserved mushroom scrapings, onion, almond flour, Parmesan, and garlic. Gently fold ingredients together and continue cooking an additional minute, then remove from heat. 3. Evenly spoon the mixture into mushroom caps and place the caps into a 6-inch round pan. Place pan into the zone 1 air fryer basket. 4. Select zone 1, select ROAST, set temperature to 190ºC, set time to 8 minutes. Then, Press START/PAUSE to begin. 5. When finished cooking, the tops will be browned and bubbling. Serve warm.

Curry Roasted Cauliflower

Prep time: 10 minutes | Cook time: 20 minutes | Serves 4

- 65 ml olive oil
- 2 teaspoons curry powder
- ½ teaspoon salt
- ¼ teaspoon freshly ground black pepper
- 1 head cauliflower, cut into bite-size florets
- ½ red onion, sliced
- 2 tablespoons freshly chopped parsley, for garnish (optional)

1. Preheat the air fryer to 200ºC. 2. In a large bowl, combine the olive oil, curry powder, salt, and pepper. Add the cauliflower and onion. Toss gently until the vegetables are completely coated with the oil mixture. Transfer the vegetables to the zone 1 and zone 2 basket of the air fryer. 3. Select zone 1, select AIR FRY, set temperature to 200ºC, set time to 20 minutes. Press MATCH COOK to match zone 2 to zone 1. Then, Press START/PAUSE to begin. Pausing about halfway through the cooking time to shake the basket. Top with the parsley, if desired, before serving.

Golden Pickles

Prep time: 10 minutes | Cook time: 15 minutes | Serves 4

- 14 dill pickles, sliced
- 30 g flour
- ⅛ teaspoon baking powder
- Pinch of salt
- 2 tablespoons cornflour plus
- 3 tablespoons water
- 6 tablespoons panko bread crumbs
- ½ teaspoon paprika
- Cooking spray

1. Preheat the air fryer to 200ºC. 2. Drain any excess moisture out of the dill pickles on a paper towel. 3. In a bowl, combine the flour, baking powder and salt. 4. Throw in the cornflour and water mixture and combine well with a whisk. 5. Put the panko bread crumbs in a shallow dish along with the paprika. Mix thoroughly. 6. Dip the pickles in the flour batter, before coating in the bread crumbs. Spritz all the pickles with the cooking spray. 7. Transfer to the zone 1 and zone 2 air fryer basket. Select zone 1, select ROAST, set temperature to 200ºC, set time to 15 minutes. Press MATCH COOK to match zone 2 to zone 1. Then, Press START/PAUSE to begin or until golden brown. 8. Serve immediately.

Garlic-Parmesan Crispy Baby Potatoes

Prep time: 10 minutes | Cook time: 15 minutes | Serves 4

- Oil, for spraying
- 450 g baby potatoes
- 45 g grated Parmesan cheese, divided
- 3 tablespoons olive oil
- 2 teaspoons garlic powder
- ½ teaspoon onion powder
- ½ teaspoon salt
- ¼ teaspoon freshly ground black pepper
- ¼ teaspoon paprika
- 2 tablespoons chopped fresh parsley, for garnish

1. Line the air fryer basket with parchment and spray lightly with oil. 2. Rinse the potatoes, pat dry with paper towels, and place in a large bowl. 3. In a small bowl, mix together 45 g of Parmesan cheese, the olive oil, garlic, onion powder, salt, black pepper, and paprika. Pour the mixture over the potatoes and toss to coat. 4. Transfer the potatoes to the prepared zone 1 and zone 2 baskets and spread them out in an even layer, taking care to keep them from touching. 5. Select zone 1, select AIR FRY, set temperature to 200°C, set time to 15 minutes. Press MATCH COOK to match zone 2 to zone 1. Then, Press START/PAUSE to begin. Stirring after 7 to 8 minutes, or until easily pierced with a fork. Continue to cook for another 1 to 2 minutes, if needed. 6. Sprinkle with the parsley and the remaining Parmesan cheese and serve.

Hasselback Potatoes with Chive Pesto

Prep time: 10 minutes | Cook time: 40 minutes | Serves 2

- 2 medium Maris Piper potatoes
- 5 tablespoons olive oil
- coarse sea salt and freshly ground black pepper, to taste
- 10 g roughly chopped fresh chives
- 2 tablespoons packed fresh flat-leaf parsley leaves
- 1 tablespoon chopped walnuts
- 1 tablespoon grated Parmesan cheese
- 1 teaspoon fresh lemon juice
- 1 small garlic clove, peeled
- 60 g sour cream

1. Place the potatoes on a cutting board and lay a chopstick or thin-handled wooden spoon to the side of each potato. Thinly slice the potatoes crosswise, letting the chopstick or spoon handle stop the blade of your knife, and stop ½ inch short of each end of the potato. Rub the potatoes with 1 tablespoon of the olive oil and season with salt and pepper. 2. Place the potatoes, cut-side up, in the zone 1 and zone 2 air fryer. 3. Select zone 1, select AIR FRY, set temperature to 190°C, set time to 40 minutes. Press MATCH COOK to match zone 2 to zone 1. Then, Press START/PAUSE to begin until golden brown and crisp on the outside and tender inside. Drizzling the insides with 1 tablespoon more olive oil and seasoning with more salt and pepper halfway through. 4. Meanwhile, in a small blender or food processor, combine the remaining 3 tablespoons olive oil, the chives, parsley, walnuts, Parmesan, lemon juice, and garlic and purée until smooth. Season the chive pesto with salt and pepper. 5. Remove the potatoes from the air fryer and transfer to plates. Drizzle the potatoes with the pesto, letting it drip down into the grooves, then dollop each with sour cream and serve hot.

Crispy Lemon Artichoke Hearts

Prep time: 10 minutes | Cook time: 15 minutes | Serves 2

- 1 (425 g) tin artichoke hearts in water, drained
- 1 egg
- 1 tablespoon water
- 30 g whole wheat bread crumbs
- ¼ teaspoon salt
- ¼ teaspoon paprika
- ½ lemon

1. Preheat the air fryer to 190°C. 2. In a medium shallow bowl, beat together the egg and water until frothy. 3. In a separate medium shallow bowl, mix together the bread crumbs, salt, and paprika. 4. Dip each artichoke heart into the egg mixture, then into the bread crumb mixture, coating the outside with the crumbs. Place the artichokes hearts in a single layer of the zone 1 air fryer basket. 5. Select zone 1, select AIR FRY, set temperature to 190°C, set time to 15 minutes. Then, Press START/PAUSE to begin. 6. Remove the artichokes from the air fryer, and squeeze fresh lemon juice over the top before serving.

Parmesan and Herb Sweet Potatoes

Prep time: 10 minutes | Cook time: 18 minutes | Serves 4

- 2 large sweet potatoes, peeled and cubed
- 65 ml olive oil
- 1 teaspoon dried rosemary
- ½ teaspoon salt
- 2 tablespoons shredded Parmesan

1. Preheat the air fryer to 180°C. 2. In a large bowl, toss the sweet potatoes with the olive oil, rosemary, and salt. 3. Pour the potatoes into the zone 1 and zone 2 air fryer baskets. Select zone 1, select ROAST, set temperature to 180°C, set time to 10 minutes. Press MATCH COOK to match zone 2 to zone 1. Then, Press START/PAUSE to begin. Stir the potatoes and sprinkle the Parmesan over the top. Continue roasting for 8 minutes more. 4. Serve hot and enjoy.

Mole-Braised Cauliflower

Prep time: 10 minutes | Cook time: 15 minutes | Serves 2

- 230 g medium cauliflower florets
- 1 tablespoon vegetable oil
- coarse sea salt and freshly ground black pepper, to taste
- 350 ml vegetable stock
- 2 tablespoons New Mexico chilli powder (or regular chilli powder)
- 2 tablespoons salted roasted peanuts
- 1 tablespoon toasted sesame seeds, plus more for garnish
- 1 tablespoon finely chopped golden raisins
- 1 teaspoon coarse sea salt
- 1 teaspoon dark brown sugar
- ½ teaspoon dried oregano
- ¼ teaspoon cayenne pepper
- ⅛ teaspoon ground cinnamon

1. In a large bowl, toss the cauliflower with the oil and season with salt and black pepper. Transfer to a cake pan. 2. Place the pan in the zone 1 air fryer. Select zone 1, select ROAST, set temperature to 190°C, set time to 10 minutes. Then, Press START/PAUSE to begin until the cauliflower is tender and lightly browned at the edges. Stirring halfway through. 3. Meanwhile, in a small blender, combine the stock, chilli powder, peanuts, sesame seeds, raisins, salt, brown sugar, oregano, cayenne, and cinnamon and purée until smooth. Pour into a small saucepan or frying pan and bring to a simmer over medium heat, then cook until reduced by half, 3 to 5 minutes. 4. Pour the hot mole sauce over the cauliflower in the pan, stir to coat, then cook until the sauce is thickened and lightly charred on the cauliflower, about 5 minutes more. Sprinkle with more sesame seeds and serve warm.

Indian Aubergine Bharta

Prep time: 15 minutes | Cook time: 20 minutes | Serves 4

- 1 medium aubergine
- 2 tablespoons vegetable oil
- 25 g finely minced onion
- 100 g finely chopped fresh tomato
- 2 tablespoons fresh lemon juice
- 2 tablespoons chopped fresh coriander
- ½ teaspoon coarse sea salt
- ⅛ teaspoon cayenne pepper

1. Rub the aubergine all over with the vegetable oil. Place the aubergine in the air fryer basket. Select zone 1, select AIR FRY, set temperature to 200°C, set time to 20 minutes. Then, Press START/PAUSE to begin until the aubergine skin is blistered and charred. 2. Transfer the aubergine to a re-sealable plastic bag, seal, and set aside for 15 to 20 minutes (the aubergine will finish cooking in the residual heat trapped in the bag). 3. Transfer the aubergine to a large bowl. Peel off and discard the charred skin. Roughly mash the aubergine flesh. Add the onion, tomato, lemon juice, coriander, salt, and cayenne. Stir to combine.

Easy Rosemary Runner Beans

Prep time: 5 minutes | Cook time: 5 minutes | Serves 1

- 1 tablespoon butter, melted
- 2 tablespoons rosemary
- ½ teaspoon salt
- 3 cloves garlic, minced
- 95 g chopped runner beans

1. Preheat the air fryer to 200°C. 2. Combine the melted butter with the rosemary, salt, and minced garlic. Toss in the runner beans, coating them well. 3. Select zone 1, select BAKE, set temperature to 200°C, set time to 5 minutes. Then, Press START/PAUSE to begin 4. Serve immediately.

Fried Brussels Sprouts

Prep time: 10 minutes | Cook time: 18 minutes | Serves 4

- 1 teaspoon plus 1 tablespoon extra-virgin olive oil, divided
- 2 teaspoons minced garlic
- 2 tablespoons honey
- 1 tablespoon sugar
- 2 tablespoons freshly squeezed lemon juice
- 2 tablespoons rice vinegar
- 2 tablespoons sriracha
- 450 g Brussels sprouts, stems trimmed and any tough leaves removed, rinsed, halved lengthwise, and dried
- ½ teaspoon salt
- Cooking oil spray

1. In a small saucepan over low heat, combine 1 teaspoon of olive oil, the garlic, honey, sugar, lemon juice, vinegar, and sriracha. Cook for 2 to 3 minutes, or until slightly thickened. Remove the pan from the heat, cover, and set aside. 2. Place the Brussels sprouts in a resealable bag or small bowl. Add the remaining olive oil and the salt, and toss to coat. 3. Insert the crisper plate into the zone 1 and zone 2 baskets, and the basket into the units. Preheat the units. Select zone 1, select AIR FRY, set temperature to 200°C, set time to 3 minutes. Press MATCH COOK to match zone 2 to zone 1. Then, Press START/PAUSE to begin. 4. Once the unit is preheated, spray the crisper plate with cooking oil. Add the Brussels sprouts to the baskets. 5. Select zone 1, select AIR FRY, set temperature to 200°C, set time to 15 minutes. Press MATCH COOK to match zone 2 to zone 1. Then, Press START/PAUSE to begin. 6. After 7 or 8 minutes, remove the baskets and shake it to toss the sprouts. Reinsert the baskets to resume cooking. 7. When the cooking is complete, the leaves should be crispy and light brown and the sprout centres tender. 8. Place the sprouts in a medium serving bowl and drizzle the sauce over the top. Toss to coat, and serve immediately.

Chapter 8 Vegetables and Sides

Tingly Chili-Roasted Broccoli

Prep time: 5 minutes | Cook time: 10 minutes | Serves 2

- 340 g broccoli florets
- 2 tablespoons Asian hot chilli oil
- 1 teaspoon ground Sichuan peppercorns (or black pepper)
- 2 garlic cloves, finely chopped
- 1 (2-inch) piece fresh ginger, peeled and finely chopped
- coarse sea salt and freshly ground black pepper, to taste

1. In a bowl, toss together the broccoli, chilli oil, Sichuan peppercorns, garlic, ginger, and salt and black pepper to taste. 2. Transfer to the zone 1 air fryer. 3. Select zone 1, select ROAST, set temperature to 190ºC, set time to 10 minutes. Then, press START/PAUSE to begin. Shaking the basket halfway through, until lightly charred and tender. Remove from the air fryer and serve warm.

Zesty Fried Asparagus

Prep time: 3 minutes | Cook time: 10 minutes | Serves 4

- Oil, for spraying
- 10 to 12 spears asparagus, trimmed
- 2 tablespoons olive oil
- 1 tablespoon garlic powder
- 1 teaspoon chilli powder
- ½ teaspoon ground cumin
- ¼ teaspoon salt

1. Line the zone 1 and zone 2 air fryer baskets with parchment and spray lightly with oil. 2. If the asparagus are too long to fit easily in the air fryer, cut them in half. 3. Place the asparagus, olive oil, garlic, chilli powder, cumin, and salt in a zip-top plastic bag, seal, and toss until evenly coated. 4. Place the asparagus in the prepared basket. 5. Select zone 1, select ROAST, set temperature to 200ºC, set time to 5 minutes. Press MATCH COOK to match zone 2 to zone 1. Then, Press START/PAUSE to begin. Flip, and cook for another 5 minutes, or until bright green and firm but tender.

Marinara Pepperoni Mushroom Pizza

Prep time: 5 minutes | Cook time: 18 minutes | Serves 4

- 4 large portobello mushrooms, stems removed
- 4 teaspoons olive oil
- 225 g marinara sauce
- 225 g shredded Mozzarella cheese
- 10 slices sugar-free pepperoni

1. Preheat the air fryer to 190ºC. 2. Brush each mushroom cap with the olive oil, one teaspoon for each cap. 3. Put on two baking sheets and bake, stem-side down, then, insert to zone 1 and zone 2. Select zone 1, select AIR FRY, set temperature to 190ºC, set time to 8 minutes. Press MATCH COOK to match zone 2 to zone 1. Then, Press START/PAUSE to begin. 4. Take out of the air fryer and divide the marinara sauce, Mozzarella cheese and pepperoni evenly among the caps. 5. Air fry for another 10 minutes until browned. 6. Serve hot.

Mediterranean Courgette Boats

Prep time: 5 minutes | Cook time: 10 minutes | Serves 4

- 1 large courgette, ends removed, halved lengthwise
- 6 grape tomatoes, quartered
- ¼ teaspoon salt
- 65 g feta cheese
- 1 tablespoon balsamic vinegar
- 1 tablespoon olive oil

1. Use a spoon to scoop out 2 tablespoons from centre of each courgette half, making just enough space to fill with tomatoes and feta. 2. Place tomatoes evenly in centres of courgette halves and sprinkle with salt. Place into ungreased zone 1 and zone 2 air fryer baskets. Select zone 1, select ROAST, set temperature to 180ºC, set time to 10 minutes. Press MATCH COOK to match zone 2 to zone 1. Then, Press START/PAUSE to begin. When done, courgette will be tender. 3. Transfer boats to a serving tray and sprinkle with feta, then drizzle with vinegar and olive oil. Serve warm.

Ricotta Potatoes

Prep time: 15 minutes | Cook time: 15 minutes | Serves 4

- 4 potatoes
- 2 tablespoons olive oil
- 110 g Ricotta cheese, at room temperature
- 2 tablespoons chopped spring onions
- 1 tablespoon roughly chopped fresh parsley
- 1 tablespoon minced coriander
- 60 g Cheddar cheese, preferably freshly grated
- 1 teaspoon celery seeds
- ½ teaspoon salt
- ½ teaspoon garlic pepper

1. Preheat the air fryer to 180ºC. 2. Pierce the skin of the potatoes with a knife. 3. Air fry in the zone 1 and zone 2 air fryer baskets. Select zone 1, select ROAST, set temperature to 180ºC, set time to 13 minutes. Press MATCH COOK to match zone 2 to zone 1. Then, Press START/PAUSE to begin. If they are not cooked through by this time, leave for 2 to 3 minutes longer. 4. In the meantime, make the stuffing by combining all the other ingredients. 5. Cut halfway into the cooked potatoes to open them. 6. Spoon equal amounts of the stuffing into each potato and serve hot.

Broccoli-Cheddar Twice-Baked Potatoes

Prep time: 10 minutes | Cook time: 46 minutes | Serves 4

- Oil, for spraying
- 2 medium Maris Piper potatoes
- 1 tablespoon olive oil
- 30 g broccoli florets
- 1 tablespoon sour cream
- 1 teaspoon garlic powder
- 1 teaspoon onion powder
- 60 g shredded Cheddar cheese

1. Line the zone 1 and zone 2 air fryer basket with parchment and spray lightly with oil. 2. Rinse the potatoes and pat dry with paper towels. Rub the outside of the potatoes with the olive oil and place them in the prepared basket. 3. Select zone 1, select AIR FRY, set temperature to 200ºC, set time to 40 minutes. Press MATCH COOK to match zone 2 to zone 1. Then, Press START/PAUSE to begin until easily pierced with a fork. Let cool just enough to handle, then cut the potatoes in half lengthwise. 4. Meanwhile, place the broccoli in a microwave-safe bowl, cover with water, and microwave on high for 5 to 8 minutes. Drain and set aside. 5. Scoop out most of the potato flesh and transfer to a medium bowl. 6. Add the sour cream, garlic, and onion powder and stir until the potatoes are mashed. 7. Spoon the potato mixture back into the hollowed potato skins, mounding it to fit, if necessary. Top with the broccoli and cheese. Return the potatoes to the basket. You may need to work in batches, depending on the size of your air fryer. 8. Select zone 1, select AIR FRY, set temperature to 200ºC, set time to 3-6 minutes. Press MATCH COOK to match zone 2 to zone 1. Then, Press START/PAUSE to begin until the cheese has melted. Serve immediately.

Parmesan-Thyme Butternut Marrow

Prep time: 15 minutes | Cook time: 20 minutes | Serves 4

- 350 g butternut marrow, cubed into 1-inch pieces (approximately 1 medium)
- 2 tablespoons olive oil
- ¼ teaspoon salt
- ¼ teaspoon garlic powder
- ¼ teaspoon black pepper
- 1 tablespoon fresh thyme
- 20 g grated Parmesan

1. Preheat the air fryer to 180ºC. 2. In a large bowl, combine the cubed marrow with the olive oil, salt, garlic powder, pepper, and thyme until the marrow is well coated. 3. Pour this mixture into the zone 1 and zone 2 air fryer basketS. Select zone 1, select ROAST, set temperature to 180ºC, set time to 10 minutes. Press MATCH COOK to match zone 2 to zone 1. Then, Press START/PAUSE to begin. Stir and roast another 8 to 10 minutes more. 4. Remove the marrow from the air fryer and toss with freshly grated Parmesan before serving.

Chiles Rellenos with Red Chile Sauce

Prep time: 20 minutes | Cook time: 20 minutes | Serves 2

Peppers:
- 2 poblano peppers, rinsed and dried
- 110 g thawed frozen or drained canned maize kernels
- 1 spring onion, sliced
- 2 tablespoons chopped fresh coriander
- ½ teaspoon coarse sea salt
- ¼ teaspoon black pepper
- 150 g grated Monterey Jack cheese

Sauce:
- 3 tablespoons extra-virgin olive oil
- 25 g finely chopped brown onion
- 2 teaspoons minced garlic
- 1 (170 g) tin tomato paste
- 2 tablespoons ancho chilli powder
- 1 teaspoon dried oregano
- 1 teaspoon ground cumin
- ½ teaspoon coarse sea salt
- 470 ml chicken stock
- 2 tablespoons fresh lemon juice
- Mexican crema or sour cream, for serving

1. For the peppers: Place the peppers in the zone 1 air fryer basket. Select zone 1, select ROAST, set temperature to 200ºC, set time to 10 minutes. Then, press START/PAUSE to begin. Turning the peppers halfway through the cooking time, until their skins are charred. Transfer the peppers to a resealable plastic bag, seal, and set aside to steam for 5 minutes. Peel the peppers and discard the skins. Cut a slit down the centre of each pepper, starting at the stem and continuing to the tip. Remove the seeds, being careful not to tear the chilli. 2. In a medium bowl, combine the maize, spring onion, coriander, salt, black pepper, and cheese; set aside. 3. Meanwhile, for the sauce: In a large frying pan, heat the olive oil over medium-high heat. Add the onion and cook, stirring, until tender, about 5 minutes. Add the garlic and cook, stirring, for 30 seconds. Stir in the tomato paste, chilli powder, oregano, and cumin, and salt. Cook, stirring, for 1 minute. Whisk in the stock and lemon juice. Bring to a simmer and cook, stirring occasionally, while the stuffed peppers finish cooking. 4. Cut a slit down the centre of each poblano pepper, starting at the stem and continuing to the tip. Remove the seeds, being careful not to tear the chilli. 5. Carefully stuff each pepper with half the maize mixture. Place the stuffed peppers in a baking pan. Place the pan in the zone 1 air fryer basket. Select zone 1, select ROAST, set temperature to 200ºC, set time to 10 minutes. Then, press START/PAUSE to begin until the cheese has melted. 6. Transfer the stuffed peppers to a serving platter and drizzle with the sauce and some crema.

Chapter 8 Vegetables and Sides

Baked Jalapeño and Cheese Cauliflower Mash

Prep time: 10 minutes | Cook time: 15 minutes | Serves 6

- 1 (340 g) steamer bag cauliflower florets, cooked according to package instructions
- 2 tablespoons salted butter, softened
- 60 g cream cheese, softened
- 120 g shredded sharp Cheddar cheese
- 20 g pickled jalapeños
- ½ teaspoon salt
- ¼ teaspoon ground black pepper

1. Prepare Cauliflower Mash: Place the cooked cauliflower florets into a food processor along with the butter, double cream, Parmesan cheese, minced garlic, salt, and pepper. Pulse twenty times until the cauliflower is smooth and all ingredients are well combined. 2. Transfer to Baking Dish: Spoon the cauliflower mash into an ungreased round nonstick baking dish. Place the dish into the air fryer basket. 3. Air Fry: Select zone 1, set the AIR FRY function, adjust the temperature to 190ºC, and set the time to 15 minutes. Press START/PAUSE to begin baking. The top will be golden brown when done. 4. Serve: Serve the cauliflower mash warm as a delicious and healthy side dish.

Crispy Garlic Sliced Aubergine

Prep time: 5 minutes | Cook time: 25 minutes | Serves 4

- 1 egg
- 1 tablespoon water
- 60 g whole wheat bread crumbs
- 1 teaspoon garlic powder
- ½ teaspoon dried oregano
- ½ teaspoon salt
- ½ teaspoon paprika
- 1 medium aubergine, sliced into ¼-inch-thick rounds
- 1 tablespoon olive oil

1. Preheat Air Fryer: Preheat the air fryer to 180ºC. 2. Prepare Breading Station: Set up two shallow bowls. In the first bowl, beat together the egg and water until frothy. In the second bowl, mix together the bread crumbs, garlic powder, oregano, salt, and paprika. 3. Coat Aubergine Slices: Dip each aubergine slice into the egg mixture, ensuring it is fully coated. Then, dip each slice into the bread crumb mixture, pressing gently to adhere the crumbs to the outside. Shake off any excess. 4. Transfer to Air Fryer: Place the well-coated aubergine slices in a single layer in the preheated zone 1 and zone 2 air fryer baskets. Drizzle the tops of the aubergine slices with the olive oil. 5. Air Fry: Select zone 1, select AIR FRY, set temperature to 180ºC, and set time to 15 minutes. Press MATCH COOK to match zone 2 setting to zone 1. Then, press START/PAUSE to begin cooking. Flip the slices halfway through the cooking time and cook for an additional 10 minutes until crispy and golden brown. 6. Serve: Serve the crispy air fried aubergine slices immediately as a delicious snack or side dish.

Parmesan Mushrooms

Prep time: 5 minutes | Cook time: 15 minutes | Serves 4

- Oil, for spraying
- 450 g shitake mushrooms, stems trimmed
- 2 tablespoons olive oil
- 2 teaspoons granulated garlic
- 1 teaspoon onion powder
- ½ teaspoon salt
- ¼ teaspoon freshly ground black pepper
- 30 g grated Parmesan cheese, divided

1. Line the zone 1 and zone 2 air fryer baskets with parchment and spray lightly with oil. 2. In a large bowl, toss the mushrooms with the olive oil, garlic, onion powder, salt, and black pepper until evenly coated. 3. Place the mushrooms in the prepared zone 1 and zone 2 baskets. 4. Select zone 1, select ROAST, set temperature to 190ºC, set time to 13 minutes. Press MATCH COOK to match zone 2 to zone 1. Then, Press START/PAUSE to begin. 5. Sprinkle half of the cheese over the mushrooms and cook for another 2 minutes. 6. Transfer the mushrooms to a serving bowl, add the remaining Parmesan cheese, and toss until evenly coated. Serve immediately.

Mexican Maize in a Cup

Prep time: 5 minutes | Cook time: 10 minutes | Serves 4

- 650 g frozen maize kernels (do not thaw)
- Vegetable oil spray
- 2 tablespoons butter
- 60 g sour cream
- 60 g mayonnaise
- 20 g grated Parmesan cheese (or feta, cotija, or queso fresco)
- 2 tablespoons fresh lemon or lime juice
- 1 teaspoon chilli powder
- Chopped fresh green onion (optional)
- Chopped fresh coriander (optional)

1. Place the maize in the bottom of the zone 1 air fryer basket and spray with vegetable oil spray. Select zone 1, select AIR FRY, set temperature to 180ºC, set time to 11 minutes. Then, Press START/PAUSE to begin. 2. Transfer the maize to a serving bowl. Add the butter and stir until melted. Add the sour cream, mayonnaise, cheese, lemon juice, and chilli powder; stir until well combined. Serve immediately with green onion and coriander (if using).

Chapter 9
Vegetarian Mains

Chapter 9 Vegetarian Mains

Baked Turnip and Courgette

Prep time: 5 minutes | Cook time: 15 to 20 minutes | Serves 4

- 3 turnips, sliced
- 1 large courgette, sliced
- 1 large red onion, cut into rings
- 2 cloves garlic, crushed
- 1 tablespoon olive oil
- Salt and black pepper, to taste

1. Preheat the Air Fryer: Preheat the air fryer to 170ºC. 2. Prepare Vegetables: Put the turnips, courgette, red onion, and garlic in a baking pan. 3. Season Vegetables: Drizzle the olive oil over the top of the vegetables and sprinkle with salt and pepper. Toss to coat evenly. 4. Air Fry Vegetables: Place the baking pan in the preheated zone 1 air fryer. Select zone 1. Set the AIR FRY function to 170ºC and bake for 15 to 20 minutes, or until the vegetables are tender, shaking the basket halfway through the cooking time. 5. Serve: Remove the vegetables from the air fryer basket and serve on a plate.

Sweet Potatoes with Courgette

Prep time: 20 minutes | Cook time: 20 minutes | Serves 4

- 2 large-sized sweet potatoes, peeled and quartered
- 1 medium courgette, sliced
- 1 Serrano or red chilli, deseeded and thinly sliced
- 1 pepper, deseeded and thinly sliced
- 1 to 2 carrots, cut into matchsticks
- 60 ml olive oil
- 1½ tablespoons maple syrup
- ½ teaspoon porcini powder or paste
- ¼ teaspoon mustard powder
- ½ teaspoon fennel seeds
- 1 tablespoon garlic powder
- ½ teaspoon fine sea salt
- ¼ teaspoon ground black pepper
- Tomato ketchup, for serving

1. Prepare the Vegetables: Put the chopped sweet potatoes, sliced courgette, chopped bell peppers, and chopped carrot into the zone 1 and zone 2 air fryer baskets. Drizzle with olive oil and toss to coat evenly. 2. Preheat the Air Fryer: Preheat the air fryer to 180ºC. 3. Air Fry the Vegetables: Place the two air fryer basket with the vegetables into zone 1 and zone 2. Select zone 1, select the AIR FRY function, set the temperature to 180ºC, and set the time to 15 minutes. Press MATCH COOK to match zone 2 setting to zone 1. Then, press START/PAUSE to begin cooking. 4. Prepare the Sauce: While the vegetables are cooking, prepare the sauce. In a bowl, vigorously whisk together the soy sauce, honey, Dijon mustard, minced garlic, ground black pepper, and dried thyme until well combined. 5. Grease a Baking Dish: Lightly grease a baking dish with a little olive oil. 6. Transfer and Coat: Once the vegetables are cooked, transfer them to the greased baking dish. Pour the prepared sauce over the vegetables and toss to coat them well. 7. Increase the Temperature and Air Fry Again: Increase the air fryer temperature to 200ºC. Place the baking dish with the coated vegetables back into the air fryer basket. Select zone 1, set the AIR FRY function, adjust the temperature to 200ºC, and set the time for an additional 5 minutes. Press MATCH COOK to match zone 2 setting to zone 1. Then, press START/PAUSE to continue cooking until the vegetables are well-coated and slightly caramelized. 8. Serve: Serve the warm, saucy vegetables immediately with a side of tomato ketchup.

Italian Baked Egg and Veggies

Prep time: 10 minutes | Cook time: 10 minutes | Serves 2

- 2 tablespoons salted butter
- 1 small courgette, sliced lengthwise and quartered
- ½ medium green pepper, seeded and diced
- 235 g fresh spinach, chopped
- 1 medium plum tomato, diced
- 2 large eggs
- ¼ teaspoon onion powder
- ¼ teaspoon garlic powder
- ½ teaspoon dried basil
- ¼ teaspoon dried oregano

1. Grease the Ramekins: Grease two ramekins with 1 tablespoon of butter each. 2. Prepare the Vegetable Mixture: In a large bowl, toss together the diced courgette, red pepper, spinach, and tomato. 3. Fill the Ramekins: Divide the vegetable mixture evenly between the two ramekins. 4. Add the Eggs and Seasonings: Crack an egg on top of the vegetable mixture in each ramekin. Sprinkle with onion powder, garlic powder, dried basil, dried oregano, salt, and freshly ground black pepper. 5. Air Fry: Place the ramekins into the zone 1 air fryer basket. Select zone 1, select AIR FRY. Set temperature to 170ºC and set time to 10 minutes, or until the eggs are set to your liking. 6. Serve: Serve the vegetable egg cups immediately while hot.

Greek Stuffed Aubergine

Prep time: 15 minutes | Cook time: 20 minutes | Serves 2

- 1 large aubergine
- 2 tablespoons unsalted butter
- ¼ medium brown onion, diced
- 60 g chopped artichoke hearts
- 235 g fresh spinach
- 2 tablespoons diced red pepper
- 120 g crumbled feta

1. Prepare the Aubergine: Slice the aubergines in half lengthwise and scoop out the flesh, leaving enough inside for the shell to remain intact. Chop the scooped-out aubergine flesh and set aside. 2. Sauté the Vegetables: In a medium frying pan over medium heat, melt the butter and add the chopped onion. Sauté until the onions begin to soften, about 3 to 5 minutes. Add the chopped aubergine flesh, artichokes, spinach, and red pepper. Continue cooking for another 5 minutes until the peppers soften and the spinach wilts. Remove from the heat and gently fold in the crumbled feta cheese. Season with salt and freshly ground black pepper to taste. 3. Stuff the Aubergine: Spoon the vegetable mixture into each aubergine shell, dividing it evenly. 4. Preheat the Air Fryer: Preheat the air fryer to 160ºC using the Air Fry function. 5. Air Fry the Stuffed Aubergine: Place the stuffed aubergine shells into the zone 1 air fryer basket. Set the air fryer to zone 1, select the AIR FRY function, adjust the temperature to 160ºC, and set the time to 20 minutes. Press START/PAUSE to begin cooking. 6. Check for Doneness: The aubergine will be tender when done. If needed, cook for an additional 2-3 minutes until the desired tenderness is achieved. 7. Serve: Serve the stuffed aubergine warm.

Fried Root Vegetable Medley with Thyme

Prep time: 10 minutes | Cook time: 22 minutes | Serves 4

- 2 carrots, sliced
- 2 potatoes, cut into chunks
- 1 swede, cut into chunks
- 1 turnip, cut into chunks
- 1 beetroot, cut into chunks
- 8 shallots, halved
- 2 tablespoons olive oil
- Salt and black pepper, to taste
- 2 tablespoons tomato pesto
- 2 tablespoons water
- 2 tablespoons chopped fresh thyme

1. Preheat the Air Fryer: Preheat the air fryer to 200ºC using the Air Fry function. 2. Prepare the Vegetables: In a large mixing bowl, toss the carrots, potatoes, swede, turnip, beetroot, and shallots with olive oil, salt, and pepper until the root vegetables are evenly coated. 3. Air Fry the Vegetables: Place the coated root vegetables in the zone 1 and zone 2 air fryer baskets. Set the air fryer to zone 1, select the AIR FRY function, adjust the temperature to 200ºC, and set the time for 12 minutes. Press MATCH COOK to match zone 2 setting to zone 1. Then, Press START/PAUSE to begin cooking. 4. Shake and Continue Cooking: After 12 minutes, shake the baskets to ensure even cooking. Continue to air fry for another 10 minutes until the vegetables are cooked to your preferred doneness. 5. Prepare the Tomato Pesto Drizzle: While the vegetables are cooking, whisk together the tomato pesto and water in a small bowl until smooth. 6. Serve the Vegetables: Once the vegetables are done, remove them from the air fryer baskets and transfer to a serving platter. Drizzle the tomato pesto mixture over the top and sprinkle with fresh thyme leaves. 7. Serve Immediately: Serve the air fried root vegetables immediately while hot.

Cheese Stuffed Courgette

Prep time: 20 minutes | Cook time: 8 minutes | Serves 4

- 1 large courgette, cut into four pieces
- 2 tablespoons olive oil
- 235 g Ricotta cheese, room temperature
- 2 tablespoons spring onions, chopped
- 1 heaping tablespoon fresh parsley, roughly chopped
- 1 heaping tablespoon coriander, minced
- 60 g Cheddar cheese, preferably freshly grated
- 1 teaspoon celery seeds
- ½ teaspoon salt
- ½ teaspoon garlic pepper

1. Preheat the Air Fryer: Preheat the air fryer to 180ºC using the Air Fry function. 2. Cook the Courgettes: Place the whole courgettes in the zone 1 and zone 2 air fryer baskets. Set the air fryer to zone 1, select the AIR FRY function, adjust the temperature to 180ºC, and set the time to 10 minutes. Press MATCH COOK to match zone 2 setting to zone 1. Then, Press START/PAUSE to begin cooking. After 10 minutes, check for doneness. If needed, cook for an additional 2-3 minutes until the courgettes are tender. 3. Prepare the Stuffing: While the courgettes are cooking, prepare the stuffing. In a medium bowl, mix together the breadcrumbs, grated Parmesan cheese, minced garlic, olive oil, dried oregano, dried basil, salt, and freshly ground black pepper until well combined. 4. Stuff the Courgettes: Once the courgettes are thoroughly cooked, carefully open them up lengthwise and scoop out a small portion of the flesh to create a hollow for the stuffing. Divide the stuffing mixture evenly among the courgette halves. 5. Bake the Stuffed Courgettes: Place the stuffed courgettes back into the air fryer baskets. Air fry at 180ºC for an additional 5 minutes until the stuffing is golden and crispy. 6. Serve: Serve the stuffed courgettes warm.

Russet Potato Gratin

Prep time: 10 minutes | Cook time: 35 minutes | Serves 6

- 120 ml milk
- 7 medium russet or Maris Piper potatoes, peeled
- Salt, to taste
- 1 teaspoon black pepper
- 120 ml double cream
- 120 g grated semi-mature cheese
- ½ teaspoon nutmeg

1. Preheat the Air Fryer: Preheat the air fryer to 200ºC using the Air Fry function. 2. Prepare the Potatoes: Cut the potatoes into wafer-thin slices. 3. Prepare the Milk Mixture: In a bowl, combine the milk and heavy cream. Sprinkle with salt, freshly ground black pepper, and ground nutmeg. Mix well. 4. Coat the Potato Slices: Use the milk mixture to coat the slices of potatoes thoroughly. 5. Assemble in Baking Dish: Arrange the coated potato slices in a baking dish. Pour the remaining milk mixture over the top of the potatoes to ensure they are well-covered. 6. Air Fry: Place the baking dish in zone 1 and zone 2 of the air fryer baskets. Set zone 1 to AIR FRY, adjust the temperature to 200ºC, and set the time to 25 minutes. Press MATCH COOK to match zone 2 setting to zone 1. Then, Press START/PAUSE to begin cooking. 7. Add Cheese and Continue Baking: After 25 minutes, check the potatoes for doneness. They should be tender and starting to brown. Pour the grated cheddar cheese over the top of the potatoes in the baking dish. Continue to air fry in the two zones for an additional 10 minutes, ensuring the top is nicely browned and the cheese is melted and bubbly before serving. 8. Serve: Remove the baking dish from the air fryer and let it cool for a few minutes. Serve the scalloped potatoes warm.

Cheesy Cauliflower Pizza Crust

Prep time: 15 minutes | Cook time: 11 minutes | Serves 2

- 1 (340 g) steamer bag cauliflower
- 120 g shredded extra mature Cheddar cheese
- 1 large egg
- 2 tablespoons blanched finely ground almond flour
- 1 teaspoon Italian blend seasoning

1. Prepare the Cauliflower: Cook the cauliflower according to the package instructions. Remove from the bag and place into cheesecloth or a paper towel to squeeze out excess water. 2. Mix Ingredients: In a large bowl, combine the drained cauliflower, grated mozzarella cheese, egg, almond flour, and Italian seasoning. Mix well until fully combined. 3. Form the Pizza Crust: Cut a piece of parchment paper to fit your air fryer basket. Press the cauliflower mixture into a 6-inch round circle on the parchment paper. 4. Preheat the Air Fryer: Preheat the air fryer to 180ºC using the Air Fry function. 5. Air Fry the Pizza Crust: Place the parchment paper with the cauliflower crust into the zone 1 air fryer basket. Set the air fryer to zone 1, select the AIR FRY function, adjust the temperature to 180ºC, and set the time to 11 minutes. Press START/PAUSE to begin cooking. After 7 minutes, carefully flip the pizza crust to ensure even cooking. 6. Add Toppings and Continue Cooking: Add your preferred pizza toppings to the partially cooked crust. Return the pizza to the air fryer basket and cook for an additional 4 minutes, or until the toppings are fully cooked and the crust is golden.

Loaded Cauliflower Steak

Prep time: 5 minutes | Cook time: 7 minutes | Serves 4

- 1 medium head cauliflower
- 60 ml hot sauce
- 2 tablespoons salted butter, melted
- 60 g blue cheese, crumbled
- 60 g full-fat ranch dressing

1. Prepare the Cauliflower: Remove the leaves from the cauliflower head. Slice the cauliflower into 1/2-inch-thick steaks. 2. Prepare the Sauce: In a small bowl, mix the hot sauce and melted butter. Brush the mixture over both sides of the cauliflower steaks. 3. Preheat the Air Fryer: Preheat the air fryer to 200ºC. 4. Air Fry the Cauliflower Steaks: Place each cauliflower steak into the zone 1 and zone 2 air fryer baskets. Set the air fryer to zone 1, select the AIR FRY function, adjust the temperature to 200ºC, and set the time to 7 minutes. Press MATCH COOK to match zone 1 setting to zone 2. Then, press START/PAUSE to begin cooking. 5. Check for Doneness: When cooked, the edges of the cauliflower steaks will begin turning dark and caramelized.

Roasted Vegetables with Rice

Prep time: 5 minutes | Cook time: 12 minutes | Serves 4

- 2 teaspoons melted butter
- 235 g chopped mushrooms
- 235 g cooked rice
- 235 g peas
- 1 carrot, chopped
- 1 red onion, chopped
- 1 garlic clove, minced
- Salt and black pepper, to taste
- 2 hard-boiled eggs, grated
- 1 tablespoon soy sauce

1. Preheat the Air Fryer: Preheat the air fryer to 190ºC. 2. Prepare Baking Dish: Coat a baking dish with melted butter. 3. Mix Ingredients: In a large bowl, stir together the mushrooms, cooked rice, peas, carrot, onion, garlic, salt, and pepper until well mixed. 4. Transfer to Air Fryer: Pour the mixture into the prepared baking dish and transfer to the zone 1 air fryer basket. 5. Roast: Select zone 1, set the AIR FRY function, set the temperature to 190ºC, and set the time to 12 minutes. Press START/PAUSE to begin roasting until the vegetables are tender. 6. Serve: Divide the mixture among four plates. Serve warm with a sprinkle of grated eggs and a drizzle of soy sauce.

Chapter 9 Vegetarian Mains

Chapter 10

Desserts

Chapter 10 Desserts

Chocolate Chip Biscuit Cake

Prep time: 5 minutes | Cook time: 15 minutes | Serves 8

- 4 tablespoons salted butter, melted
- 65 g granular brown sweetener
- 1 large egg
- ½ teaspoon vanilla extract
- 55 g blanched finely ground almond flour
- ½ teaspoon baking powder
- 40 g low-carb chocolate crisps

1. In a large bowl, whisk together butter, sweetener, egg, and vanilla. Add flour and baking powder and stir until combined. 2. Fold in chocolate crisps, then spoon batter into an ungreased round nonstick baking dish. 3. Place dish into zone 1 air fryer basket. Place the baking pan into the preheated zone 1 air fryer basket. Select zone 1, select BAKE, set temperature to 150ºC and set time to 15 minutes. Then, press START/PAUSE to begin. When edges are browned, biscuit cake will be done. 4. Slice and serve warm.

Sweet Potato Donut Holes

Prep time: 10 minutes | Cook time: 4 to 5 minutes per batch | Makes 18 donut holes

- 65 g Plain flour
- 50 g granulated sugar
- ¼ teaspoon baking soda
- 1 teaspoon baking powder
- ⅛ teaspoon salt
- 125 g cooked & mashed purple sweet potatoes
- 1 egg, beaten
- 2 tablespoons butter, melted
- 1 teaspoon pure vanilla extract
- Coconut, or avocado oil for misting or cooking spray

1. Preheat the Air Fryer: Insert the crisper plate into the zone 1 and zone 2 air fryer baskets and then insert the baskets into the units. Preheat the air fryer to 200ºC. 2. Prepare the Dry Ingredients: In a large bowl, stir together the flour, granulated sugar, baking soda, baking powder, and salt until well combined. 3. Prepare the Wet Ingredients: In a separate bowl, combine the mashed potatoes, egg, melted butter, and vanilla extract. Mix well until smooth and fully incorporated. 4. Combine Wet and Dry Ingredients: Add the potato mixture to the dry ingredients. Stir until a soft dough forms. The dough should be slightly sticky but manageable. 5. Shape the Dough: Lightly flour your hands and shape the dough into 1½-inch balls. Place the dough balls on a baking sheet or plate. 6. Prepare for Air Frying: Lightly mist the dough balls with cooking spray or oil to ensure they crisp up nicely in the air fryer. 7. Air Fry the Donut Holes: Place donut holes into the preheated zone 1 and zone 2 air fryer baskets, leaving a little space between each ball to allow for even cooking. Select zone 1, select BAKE, set temperature 200ºC and set time to 4-5 minutes. Press MATCH COOK to match zone 2 setting to zone 1. Then, press START/PAUSE to begin. The donut holes should be golden brown on the outside and cooked through in the center. Carefully remove the cooked donut holes from the air fryer and let them cool on a wire rack. 8. Serve: Serve the warm potato donut holes plain or with your favorite dipping sauce or glaze.

Vanilla Pound Cake

Prep time: 10 minutes | Cook time: 25 minutes | Serves 6

- 55 g blanched finely ground almond flour
- 55 g salted butter, melted
- 100 g granulated sweetener
- 1 teaspoon vanilla extract
- 1 teaspoon baking powder
- 120 ml full-fat sour cream
- 30 full-fat cream cheese, softened
- 2 large eggs

1. In a large bowl, mix the almond flour, melted butter, and granulated sweetener until well combined. Add in the vanilla extract, baking powder, sour cream, and cream cheese. Mix until smooth and fully incorporated. Add the eggs and mix until the batter is well combined and smooth. 2. Preheat the air fryer to 150ºC. 3. Pour Batter into Pan: Pour the batter into a round baking pan that fits into zone 1 air fryer basket. Smooth the top with a spatula if needed.
Bake the Cake: Place the baking pan into the preheated zone 1 air fryer basket. Select zone 1, select BAKE, set temperature to 150ºC and set time to 25 minutes. Then, press START/PAUSE to begin. 4. Check for Doneness: After 25 minutes, check the cake by inserting a toothpick into the center. If it comes out clean and the center feels firm (not wet), the cake is done. If necessary, cook for an additional 2-3 minutes. 5. Cool the Cake: Allow the cake to cool completely in the pan before attempting to move it. This will help prevent crumbling. 6. Serve: Once cooled, carefully remove the cake from the pan. Serve as desired.

Berry Crumble

Prep time: 10 minutes | Cook time: 15 minutes | Serves 4

For the Filling:
- 300 g mixed berries
- 2 tablespoons sugar
- 1 tablespoon cornflour
- 1 tablespoon fresh lemon juice

For the Topping:
- 15 g Plain flour
- 20 g rolled oats
- 1 tablespoon granulated sugar
- 2 tablespoons cold unsalted butter, cut into small cubes
- Whipped cream or ice cream (optional)

1. Preheat the air fryer to 200ºC. 2. For the filling: In a round baking pan, gently mix the berries, sugar, cornflour, and lemon juice until thoroughly combined. 3. For the topping: In a small bowl, combine the flour, oats, and sugar. Stir the butter into the flour mixture until the mixture has the consistency of breadcrumbs. 4. Sprinkle the topping over the berries. 5. Put the pan in the zone 1 air fryer basket. Select zone 1, select BAKE, set temperature to 200ºC, set time to 15 minutes. Then, press START/PAUSE to begin. Let cool for 5 minutes on a wire rack. 6. Serve topped with whipped cream or ice cream, if desired.

Rhubarb and Strawberry Crumble

Prep time: 10 minutes | Cook time: 12 to 17 minutes | Serves 6

- 250 g sliced fresh strawberries
- 95 g sliced rhubarb
- 40 g granulated sugar
- 30 g quick-cooking porridge
- 25 g whole-wheat pastry flour, or Plain flour
- 40 g packed light brown sugar
- ½ teaspoon ground cinnamon
- 3 tablespoons unsalted butter, melted

1. Prepare the Air Fryer: Insert the crisper plate into the air fryer basket and then insert the basket into the unit. Preheat the air fryer to 190ºC. 2. Prepare the Fruit Filling: In a 6-by-2-inch round metal baking pan, combine the strawberries, rhubarb, and granulated sugar. Mix well to ensure the fruit is evenly coated with sugar. 3. Prepare the Crumble Topping: In a medium bowl, stir together the porridge oats, flour, brown sugar, and ground cinnamon. Add the melted butter and stir until the mixture becomes crumbly. 4. Assemble the Crumble: Sprinkle the crumble mixture evenly over the fruit in the baking pan. 5. Air Fry the Crumble: Once the air fryer is preheated, place the baking pan into the zone 1 air fryer basket. Select zone 1, select BAKE, Set temperature to 190ºC set time to 12 minutes. Press START/PAUSE to begin. 6. Check for Doneness: After 12 minutes, check the crumble. If the fruit is bubbling and the topping is golden brown, it is done. If not, continue cooking for a few more minutes until the desired doneness is reached. 7. Serve: When the cooking is complete, remove the crumble from the air fryer and let it cool slightly. Serve warm.

Homemade Mint Pie

Prep time: 15 minutes | Cook time: 25 minutes | Serves 2

- 1 tablespoon instant coffee
- 2 tablespoons almond butter, softened
- 2 tablespoons granulated sweetener
- 1 teaspoon dried mint
- 3 eggs, beaten
- 1 teaspoon dried spearmint
- 4 teaspoons coconut flour
- Cooking spray

1. Spray the zone 1 air fryer basket with cooking spray. 2. Then mix all ingredients in the mixer bowl. 3. When you get a smooth mixture, transfer it in the zone 1 air fryer basket. Flatten it gently. Select zone 1, select BAKE, set temperature to 190ºC, set time to 25 minutes. Then, press START/PAUSE to begin.

Peaches and Apple Crumble

Prep time: 10 minutes | Cook time: 10 to 12 minutes | Serves 4

- 2 peaches, peeled, pitted, and chopped
- 1 apple, peeled and chopped
- 2 tablespoons honey
- 45 g quick-cooking oats
- 25 g whole-wheat pastry, or All-purpose flour
- 2 tablespoons unsalted butter, at room temperature
- 3 tablespoons packed brown sugar
- ½ teaspoon ground cinnamon

1. Preheat the air fryer to 190ºC. 2. Mix together the peaches, apple, and honey in a baking pan until well incorporated. 3. In a bowl, combine the oats, pastry flour, butter, brown sugar, and cinnamon and stir to mix well. Spread this mixture evenly over the fruit. 4. Place the baking pan in the zone 1 air fryer basket. Select zone 1, select BAKE, set temperature to 190ºC, set time to 10-12 minutes. Then, press START/PAUSE to begin until the fruit is bubbling around the edges and the topping is golden brown. 5. Remove from the basket and serve warm.

Chapter 10 Desserts

Coconut Muffins

Prep time: 5 minutes | Cook time: 25 minutes | Serves 5

- 55 g coconut flour
- 2 tablespoons cocoa powder
- 3 tablespoons granulated sweetener
- 1 teaspoon baking powder
- 2 tablespoons coconut oil
- 2 eggs, beaten
- 50 g desiccated coconut

1. In the mixing bowl, mix all ingredients. 2. Then pour the mixture into the moulds of the muffin and transfer in the zone 1 and zone 2 air fryer baskets. 3. Select zone 1, select BAKE, set temperature to 180°C, set time to 25 minutes. Press MATCH COOK to match zone 2 setting to zone 1. Then, press START/PAUSE to begin.

Kentucky Chocolate Nut Pie

Prep time: 20 minutes | Cook time: 25 minutes | Serves 8

- 2 large eggs, beaten
- 75 g unsalted butter, melted
- 160 g granulated sugar
- 30 g Plain flour
- 190 g coarsely chopped pecans
- 170 g milk chocolate crisps
- 2 tablespoons bourbon, or peach juice
- 1 (9-inch) unbaked piecrust

1. In a large bowl, stir together the eggs and melted butter. Add the sugar and flour and stir until combined. Stir in the pecans, chocolate crisps, and bourbon until well mixed. 2. Using a fork, prick holes in the bottom and sides of the pie crust. Pour the pie filling into the crust. 3. Preheat the air fryer to 180°C. Insert into zone 1. 4. Select zone 1, Select BAKE, set temperature to 180°C, set time to 25 minutes. Then, press START/PAUSE to begin. Or until a knife inserted into the middle of the pie comes out clean. Let set for 5 minutes before serving.

Protein Powder Doughnut Holes

Prep time: 25 minutes | Cook time: 6 minutes | Makes 12 holes

- 25g blanched finely ground almond flour
- 30 g low-carb vanilla protein powder
- 100 g granulated sweetener
- ½ teaspoon baking powder
- 1 large egg
- 5 tablespoons unsalted butter, melted
- ½ teaspoon vanilla extract

1. Mix all ingredients in a large bowl. Place into the freezer for 20 minutes. 2. Wet your hands with water and roll the dough into twelve balls. 3. Cut a piece of baking paper to fit your air fryer basket. Place doughnut holes into the zone 1 and zone 2 air fryer basket on top of baking paper. 4. Select zone 1, select BAKE, set temperature to 190°C, set time to 6 minutes. Press MATCH COOK to match zone 2 setting to zone 1. Then. Press START/PAUSE to begin. 5. Flip doughnut holes halfway through the cooking time. 6. Let cool completely before serving.

Appendix 1: Basic Kitchen Conversions & Equivalents

DRY MEASUREMENTS CONVERSION CHART

3 teaspoons = 1 tablespoon = 1/16 cup

6 teaspoons = 2 tablespoons = 1/8 cup

12 teaspoons = 4 tablespoons = 1/4 cup

24 teaspoons = 8 tablespoons = 1/2 cup

36 teaspoons = 12 tablespoons = 3/4 cup

48 teaspoons = 16 tablespoons = 1 cup

METRIC TO US COOKING CONVERSIONS

OVEN TEMPERATURES

120 °C = 250 °F

160 °C = 320 °F

180 °C = 350 °F

205 °C = 400 °F

220 °C = 425 °F

LIQUID MEASUREMENTS CONVERSION CHART

8 fluid ounces = 1 cup = 1/2 pint = 1/4 quart

16 fluid ounces = 2 cups = 1 pint = 1/2 quart

32 fluid ounces = 4 cups = 2 pints = 1 quart = 1/4 gallon

128 fluid ounces = 16 cups = 8 pints = 4 quarts = 1 gallon

BAKING IN GRAMS

1 cup flour = 140 grams

1 cup sugar = 150 grams

1 cup powdered sugar = 160 grams

1 cup heavy cream = 235 grams

VOLUME

1 milliliter = 1/5 tsp

5 ml = 1 tsp

15 ml = 1 tbsp

240 ml = 1 cup or 8 fluid ounces

1 liter = 34 fluid ounces

WEIGHT

1 gram = 0.035 ounces

100 grams = 3.5 ounces

500 grams = 1.1 pounds

1 kilogram = 35 ounces

Appendix 2: Recipes Index

A

Air Fried Chicken Potatoes with Sun-Dried Tomato	46
Air Fried Shishito Peppers	18
Air Fried Spicy Olives	53
All-in-One Toast	8
Almond and Caraway Crust Steak	24
Almond Catfish	35
Almond-Crusted Chicken	48
Apple Pie Egg Rolls	14
Apricot-Glazed Turkey Tenderloin	43
Asian Glazed Meatballs	23
Asparagus and Pepper Strata & Easy Banger Pizza	10
Avocado and Egg Burrito	14

B

Bacon Cheese Egg with Avocado & Blueberry Cobbler	9
Bacon Lovers' Stuffed Chicken	45
Bacon Pinwheels	18
Bacon Wrapped Pork with Apple Gravy	29
Bacon-Wrapped A Pickled Gherkin Spear	51
Bacon-Wrapped Hot Dogs with Mayo-Ketchup Sauce	21
Bacon-Wrapped Pork Tenderloin	25
Bacon-Wrapped Vegetable Kebabs	28
Baked Chorizo Scotch Eggs	17
Baked Egg and Mushroom Cups	5
Baked Jalapeño and Cheese Cauliflower Mash	62
Baked Potato Breakfast Boats	6
Baked Turnip and Courgette	64
Balsamic Brussels Sprouts	57
Balsamic Tilapia	35
Banger-Stuffed Mushroom Caps	57
Barbecue Chicken and Coleslaw Tostadas	44
Barbecue Ribs	28
Beef and Mango Skewers	52
Beef Bavette Steak with Sage	30
Beef Bratwursts	17
Berry Crumble	69
Blackened Red Snapper	34
Bone-in Pork Chops	23
Breaded Turkey Cutlets	48
Breakfast Cobbler	7
Breakfast Meatballs	5
Broccoli Cheese Chicken	43
Broccoli-Cheddar Twice-Baked Potatoes	61
Bruschetta Chicken	42
Bruschetta with Basil Pesto	50

C

Cajun Catfish Cakes with Cheese	35
Cantonese BBQ Pork	29
Carrot Chips	55
Catfish Bites	36
Cheddar Bacon Burst with Spinach	26
Cheese Crusted Chops	27
Cheese Stuffed Courgette	65
Cheesy Cauliflower Pizza Crust	66
Cheesy Jalapeño Cornbread	17
Cheesy Low-Carb Lasagna & Kielbasa and Cabbage	22
Chicken Hand Pies	47
Chicken Legs with Leeks	44
Chicken Parmesan	45
Chicken with Bacon and Tomato	44
Chicken with Pineapple and Peach	48
Chiles Rellenos with Red Chile Sauce	61
chilli Lime Prawns	33
Chilli Prawns	32
Chimichanga Breakfast Burrito	6
Chipotle Aioli Wings	42
Chipotle Drumsticks	45
Chocolate Chip Biscuit Cake	68
Chorizo and Beef Burger	21
Cinnamon-Raisin Bagels	9
Coconut Muffins	70
Coconut Prawns with Spicy Dipping Sauce	36
Cornish Hens with Honey-Lime Glaze	43
Crab Cakes	37
Crispy Chilli Chickpeas	55
Crispy Filo Artichoke Triangles	53
Crispy Garlic Sliced Aubergine	62
Crispy Green Tomato Slices	51
Crispy Lemon Artichoke Hearts	58
Crunchy Basil White Beans	54
Cucumber and Salmon Salad	32

Curry Roasted Cauliflower — 57

D

Drop Biscuits — 6

E

Easy Buttermilk Biscuits — 5
Easy Devils on Horseback — 17
Easy Rosemary Runner Beans — 59
Easy Spiced Nuts — 52
Easy Turkey Tenderloin — 41
Egg in a Hole — 6
Eggy Bread Sticks — 8

F

Fiesta Chicken Plate — 42
Fish Cakes — 37
Fish Gratin — 35
Fish Sandwich with Tartar Sauce — 34
Fried Brussels Sprouts — 59
Fried Catfish with Dijon Sauce — 38
Fried Green Tomatoes — 15
Fried Root Vegetable Medley with Thyme — 65

G

Garlic Balsamic London Broil — 30
Garlic-Parmesan Crispy Baby Potatoes — 58
Garlic-Roasted Tomatoes and Olives — 50
Golden Chicken Cutlets — 46
Golden Onion Rings — 54
Golden Pickles — 57
Greek Stuffed Aubergine — 65

H

Ham Chicken with Cheese — 42
Ham with Sweet Potatoes — 25
Hasselback Potatoes with Chive Pesto — 58
Herb-Crusted Lamb Chops — 27
Herbed Green Lentil Rice Balls — 51
Herbed Lamb Steaks — 26
Herbed Prawns Pita — 33
Homemade Mint Pie — 69

Honey-Apricot Muesli with Greek Yoghurt — 9
Honey-Baked Pork Loin — 24
Honey-Balsamic Salmon — 34

I

Indian Aubergine Bharta — 59
Indian Fennel Chicken — 41
Italian Baked Egg and Veggies — 64

J

Jalapeño Popper Egg Cups — 8

K

Kentucky Chocolate Nut Pie — 70

L

Lamb Burger with Feta and Olives — 26
Lemon Thyme Roasted Chicken — 44
Lemon-Basil Turkey Breasts — 46
Lemon-Blueberry Muffins — 11
Lemon-Pepper Trout — 36
Lemony Endive in Curried Yoghurt — 52
Loaded Cauliflower Steak — 66

M

Marinara Pepperoni Mushroom Pizza — 60
Meatball Subs — 14
Mediterranean Beef Steaks — 25
Mediterranean Courgette Boats — 60
Mediterranean Stuffed Chicken Breasts — 47
Meringue Cookies — 14
Mexican Maize in a Cup — 62
Mixed Vegetables Pot Stickers — 52
Mole-Braised Cauliflower — 59
Mongolian-Style Beef — 29
Mushroom and Green Bean Casserole — 13

N

New Orleans-Style Crab Cakes — 32
Nice Goulash — 45
Nigerian Peanut-Crusted Bavette Steak — 22

O

Onion Omelette	10

P

Parmesan and Herb Sweet Potatoes	58
Parmesan Mushrooms	62
Parmesan-Thyme Butternut Marrow	61
Peaches and Apple Crumble	69
Pepper Steak	27
Pepperoni Pizza Dip	53
Peppery Brown Rice Fritters	18
Personal Cauliflower Pizzas	15
Pesto Fish Pie	38
Pork and Tricolor Vegetables Kebabs	30
Pork Schnitzels with Sour Cream and Dill Sauce	23
Potato-Crusted Chicken	46
Potatoes Lyonnaise	8
Prawns Egg Rolls	50
Protein Powder Doughnut Holes	70
Puffed Egg Tarts	13
Purple Potato Chips with Rosemary	18

Q

Quick and Easy Blueberry Muffins	7

R

Rhubarb and Strawberry Crumble	69
Ricotta Potatoes	60
Roasted Halibut Steaks with Parsley	36
Roasted Vegetables with Rice	66
Russet Potato Gratin	66

S

Salmon Fritters with Courgette	38
Savoury Prawns	33
Scallops with Green Vegetables	15
Sea Bass with Avocado Cream	37
Sesame-Crusted Tuna Steak	35
Simple Scotch Eggs	5
South Indian Fried Fish	39
Southwest Corn and Pepper Roast	19
Spicy Air Fried Old Bay Shrimp	32
Spicy Chicken Bites	51
Spicy Lamb Sirloin Chops & Air Fried Broccoli	21
Spinach and Mushroom Mini Quiche	7
Steamed Tuna with Lemongrass	34
Strawberry Toast	10
Stuffed Figs with Goat Cheese and Honey	53
Sweet Chili Spiced Chicken	41
Sweet Potato Donut Holes	68
Sweet Potatoes with Courgette	64

T

Teriyaki Chicken Thighs with Lemony Mangetouts	47
Teriyaki Rump Steak with Broccoli and Capsicum	24
Teriyaki Shrimp Skewers	38
Thai Curry Meatballs	48
Thai Prawn Skewers with Peanut Dipping Sauce	33
Tingly Chili-Roasted Broccoli	60
Tomato and Cheddar Rolls	11
Tuna Steak	37
Turkey Burger Sliders	54

V

Vanilla Muesli	10
Vanilla Pound Cake	68
Veggie Tuna Melts	13
Vietnamese "Shaking" Beef	28

Y

Yellow Curry Chicken Thighs with Peanuts	43

Z

Zesty Fried Asparagus	60

Printed in Great Britain
by Amazon